Once upon a time...

Stories and drama to use in direct work with adopted and fostered children

Joan Moore

Published by
British Association for Adoption & Fostering
(BAAF)
Saffron House
6-10 Kirby Street
London EC1N 8TS

www.baaf.org.uk

Charity registration 275689 (England and Wales) and SC039337 (Scotland)

British Library Cataloguing in Publication Data
A catalogue record for this book is available from the British Library

ISBN 978 1 907585 56 2

Project management by Shaila Shah, Director of Publications, BAAF
Designed and typeset by Helen Joubert Design
Printed in Great Britain by the Lavenham Press

BAAF is the leading UK-wide membership organisation for all those concerned with adoption, fostering and child care issues.

Contents

List of story titles

Foreword

I am honoured to be asked to write this foreword, as I have been waiting with enthusiasm for Joan's book to be completed since I first heard about her plan to write it. This book, on the use of stories and creative ideas for children in foster or adoptive families, is much needed by both parents and professionals. The vast majority of these children have had profoundly traumatic histories, and they need help to play and thus make sense of their lives. Stories and creative ways of engaging their interest can really help.

I have had the pleasure of knowing Joan Moore, a fellow dramatherapist, for many years. As someone who works with this population of children and their foster and adoptive families, as Joan does, I have the highest professional regard for her: she has so much to offer both professional colleagues in our field as well as the children and families themselves.

The book is packed full of a wonderful array of ideas, and beautifully structured to enable ease in finding one's way around it. It begins with an outline of why stories might be helpful and then moves on to give clear story structures; ways that such stories could be developed further; equipment to gather for the eventuality in which a story might emerge at random within a meeting with a child; and case studies. The case studies are moving and pertinent, demonstrating the value of stories and the way that they can be used to explore a range of difficult thoughts and feelings. They also highlight how, for some children, the story is sometimes sufficient in itself, and no link to its meaning is necessary. The case studies show how, on other occasions, children welcome the opportunity to explore the links between the created story and their own "story". Another important aspect of the book is the way in which it not only provides stories that the reader can use on particular topics, but it shows the reader how to create a story from scratch or how to use a well-known story, such as a fairy story, to help a child. The final section of the book goes on to show how dilemmas past and present and particular issues can be directly explored with a child using the story structure and how profoundly helpful this can be.

From my own experience as a dramatherapist at Family Futures, working with traumatised children who are fostered or adopted, I have been inspired by all the children and the families I have worked with in their ability to use the arts to heal. We all need to tell the stories of our lives, and it is in this storytelling that we can begin to bear our stories and make sense of our experiences. It is in this process of telling and, crucially, being witnessed in our telling, that we find ways of moving forward in our lives. Storytelling is a time-honoured tradition from our own culture and from other cultures, a way in which human beings have left their mark and handed on their experiences from one generation to the next. It is lovely to have such a tradition honoured and shared in this rich and diverse guide to storytelling that is easily accessible and a pleasure to read. I cannot recommend it too highly.

Jay Vaughan
Dramatherapist and Family Futures Therapy Services Manager

Using creative activity to engage children

This is a book of stories and ideas for creative play and drama to engage insecure children whose traumatic experiences make it difficult for them to cope with change and who need help to attach to adoptive parents or foster carers. In the fast pace of our contemporary lives, people often complain that they haven't enough time or lack the confidence to create stories or to engage children in creative activity. But stories are easy to put together and creative activity can reap highly worthwhile rewards. This book will equip you to do this imaginatively and confidently.

Stories – a catalyst for change

The wisdom of older people, with their intrinsic store of knowledge and history, has traditionally been communicated through stories, mainly orally. Stories are handed down, told and retold, and always serve to enthral. They also serve to help the listener to engage and learn. The roots and value of storytelling are eloquently explained by Alida Gersie and Nancy King.

The word story has come to imply a narrative, an account of events. Its etymological roots link to a Greek word, which means to know. Tale finds its basis in "taal", language or speech (talk). Thus both story and tale reflect and indicate our ability to use language to gain knowledge of life and to communicate the process of inquiry and outcome. Stories and tales are the product, the end and therefore, paradoxically, the beginning of our journey towards understanding. (Gersie and King, 1990, p.31)

Stories and storytelling encourage children to find solutions to their dilemmas through their engagement and empathy with the characters, whose experiences children connect with their own inner conflicts, which previously seemed irresolvable. Fairy tales and myths, for example, offer the escapism of being fantasies that have no obvious relation to the real world. Yet the symbols in these stories can carry special significance for children in care, a theme expanded on later in this book. In these tales, the heroes are beset by familiar dilemmas in which they have to balance the tension between deciding whether to follow their feelings or be governed by reason, when these two are at odds. Stories can promote the message to "keep trying", their themes inspiring children not to give up. In our desire to resolve problems, we can be tempted to focus solely on the "end goal"; however, case examples throughout the book demonstrate that the process of change entered by creating stories is in itself valuable for its potentially transformative effects. This is because stories and play act as catalysts for change through engaging the senses, imagination and memory.

Historical perspectives

The last century has brought a wealth of knowledge to our understanding of play as essential to children's healthy development. Of particular renown is psychiatrist Jacob Moreno (1946), inventor of psychodrama. From seeing children communicate spontaneously through play, Moreno encouraged his patients to act out their problems theatrically. Sigmund Freud (1948), too, recognised the importance of play in building relationships. In the process of developing "talk therapy" he alighted on dreams as a "royal road" to the unconscious. Carl Jung (1968), once a pupil of Freud, linked the symbols in dreams to universal "archetypes".

Exploring symbols that emerge in play can give useful insights into a child's personality and experience. For example, while a "horse" may symbolise power for a child, an "ant", although tiny, can mobilise armies! Chapter 1, in describing how to tell stories, gives a list of symbols that feature in the play of traumatised children, alongside the possible meanings these might have for them. In his seminal work, *Child Drama*, Peter Slade (1954) described the profound influence that children's experiments in play and drama had on their emotional and social development. Optimal development, of course, is helped by early nurture.

During the 1950s, Bowlby and Ainsworth (1962) observed infants to have a built-in signalling system to elicit nurture and protection from their mothers. From Bowlby's research on the impact of separation of young children from their mothers, he developed his theory of attachment, which became socio-politically unpopular in a decade when women were taking up careers and placing their children in nurseries. Since then, discoveries in neuroscience (notably Siegel, 1999; Perry and Szalavitz, 2006; and Cozolino, 2006) that have clarified children's need for nurture, comfort and the freedom to play, evidence how pertinent Bowlby's theory is. Building on these findings, Professor Sue Jennings, dramatherapist and anthropologist, has developed her model of neuro-dramatic play. She explains why dramatic play, particularly, is so vital for children:

It is only through being able to play dramatically, to take on roles in thought or action, that we are able to consider the feelings and experiences of somebody else. This is how we develop empathy and the child who cannot engage in dramatic playing will have great difficulty with understanding the "other". (Jennings, 2011, p.30)

Emotional deprivation

Infants learn of their right to be in the world from mirroring interactions in which nurturing mothers reflect and magnify their baby's expressions. Peter Fonagy (2009) describes the mothers who are able to take their child's psychological perspective as "mind minded". In play, substitute parents can replicate this important bonding interaction that neglected children so often miss. Chapter 5 outlines the principles of my "Theatre of Attachment" model, which involves adoptive parents and foster carers in re-enactment of their children's history. Case examples include plays that illustrate the shared emotional experience that this method invites (also, see Moore, 2006, 2008, 2010).

Sadly, the birth parents of many children adopted from public care in the UK do not have this nurturing ability. Rather, they just react to events without thinking or planning (Perry and Szalavitz, 2006), their lives being steeped in extraordinary drama that they continually create, as though to convince themselves that they exist. About the drama of family life, MacIntyre has said:

We enter upon a stage which we did not design and we find ourselves part of an action that was not of our making. Each of us being a main character in his/her own drama plays subordinate parts in the drama of others and each drama constrains the others. (MacIntyre, 1985, p.213)

Emotionally fragile children who are deprived of comfort in their early years grow to believe that they do not deserve love. In their foster and adoptive families they can recreate the chaotic, destructive relationships that necessitated their removal to safer care. Yet, as Bowlby (1973) warned, separation from their parent is the ultimate threat for young children. Being moved to new sets of carers will accelerate their loss of any sense of prediction and will affect their ability to cope with uncertainty and change. Accommodating to a new culture can oblige the child to develop a different identity, even before their future is decided. Barratt and Granville advise that:

Helping to maintain a sense of connection with the past and the origin of the self by telling stories and creating rituals is important for adopted children and an important factor in developing a new family identity. (Barratt, 2006, p.160)

The stories in Chapter 2 help such children to rebuild their identity; set in fictional contexts, such as the jungle, they illustrate equivalent predicaments in which the central character masters adversity and reconciles to change, showing how brave the hero is, so as to inspire courage and hope in the child.

Despite their troubled backgrounds, some children can also show remarkable resilience. The impressive progress they make, as a result of improved standards of care in their adoptive families, is evidenced in research by Rushton (2003).

Case examples in Chapter 6 demonstrate the processing and resolution of complex feelings by children through dramatic play. Collishaw *et al* (2007) found that a substantial minority of abused children who were subsequently adopted did not have mental health problems in adult life, making it difficult to predict with certainty which problems will progress into adulthood.

Still, as Ironside (2004) comments, children's fear-based reactions can engender panic in adults who, in trying to respond with empathy, feel rebuffed and useless. Rushton defines the challenges that abused children present, including:

...conduct problems (impulsivity, over-activity, oppositional behaviour, attentional problems and temper tantrums, and sometimes serious aggression), as well as disturbed attachment patterns or slowness to attach to new carers, indiscriminate sociability and lack of trust. (Rushton, 2010, p.39)

These problems are hardly surprising given that so many will have experienced or witnessed violence, perpetrated mainly against their mothers. Indeed, Hester (2011) expresses concern about the coercive, controlling behaviour of aggressive men in domestically violent relationships and the inherent gender inequalities implicit in how the system responds, especially to mothers. Children imitate their parents, and in order to survive in violent contexts, they become untrusting, aggressive and dismissive. Such problems can make us question why, in the face of persistent rejection, we keep trying so hard to understand children who deny their need for relationships. Ethological explanations of how the human brain evolved serve to show why attachment is so integral to human survival:

Without others we could not survive in the natural world. Then and today the presence of familiar people projecting the social emotional cues of acceptance, compassion, caring and safety calms the stress response of the individual. (Perry, 2009, p.246)

Cultural groups who live and socialise across the generations and have the lowest rates of crime and mental ill health further evidence the advantages of social cohesion. In contrast, the families of children in public care tend to be socially isolated, with inadequate support from relatives and acquaintances.

During the 1960s, when research on attachment began to proliferate, 70 per cent of individuals were estimated to be "securely attached", yet by 2006, this figure had fallen to 55 per cent (Kenrick *et al*, 2006). Since whole communities have survived natural disasters by mobilising their people to escape to safer territory (Crittenden, 2009), it seems that to have organised strategies and be in relationships and able to read people's faces is conducive to survival. Problems arise when (for an estimated 15 per cent of the population) their strategies become maladaptive and lead to or involve substance dependency, mental illness and violence.

The problems of the rising proportion of these insecurely attached individuals, especially in the West, are attributed to the higher incidence of distress, drug addiction and violence (Kessler *et al*, 2003; Kawakami *et al*, 2004). In Eastern cultures, required commitment on the part of individuals to the family group appears to afford greater protection. The primal need for comfort is illustrated by Harlow's (1951) research on bereaved monkeys, who preferred the soft comfort dummy to the wire one to which their food was attached.

Irrespective of their culture or heritage, young infants raise or inhibit their needs when their parents are unresponsive. As Rushton (2010) comments, debate continues over the concepts and categorisation of attachment behaviour. Critics of attachment theory argue that adult–child interactions need interpretations to take broader account of cultural differences, subtle variations in personality, child development and attitudes to childhood. For example, Murphy (2007) noted that while some parents regard young children as a "blank sheet" on which quality of care determines outcome, others perceive them to be deliberately manipulative, taking the view that the child has to be trained to conform from the very beginning. Still, in the absence of a comprehensive alternative, attachment theory provides a framework that helps explain complex, challenging behaviour. Selwyn (2010, p.35) asserts that:

We need a shift in focus to prioritising children's relationships and their need for stable secure relationships back to the top of the hierarchy of need.

Special needs and the effects of trauma

Increasingly, children in care are found to have highly complex needs. In their study of 300 children, aged 3–11 years, Selwyn *et al* (2006) reported that by the time an "adoption in best interests" decision was made, 95 per cent of the children had at least one special need – health, developmental or emotional; 50 per cent had four or more special needs; and of the 96 children eventually placed for adoption, only one quarter of them were free of serious difficulties.

The problems often begin before the child is born, the foetus being especially vulnerable to drug and alcohol misuse. O'Connor and Paley (2006) found that the more alcohol the mother drank in pregnancy, the smaller her baby's head circumference and the more depressive symptoms seen in her children at 4–5 years. Increasing numbers of babies in the UK are born drug addicted and grow up to have multiple long-term problems (Brocklesby *et al*, 2009; Mukherjee, 2009). According to Kolb *et al* (2003, p.109), during gestation, neurons generate at a rate of around 250,000 per minute and in the first six months after birth the infant's brain continues to develop at astonishing speed. This growth can be stunted if the child is subjected to traumatic experiences.

Perry and Szalavitz (2006) describe how trauma causes this myelin insulation to become eroded by excessive chemicals, which, as Sunderland (2007) explains, severs connections and leaves the highly distressed child totally unable to self-soothe. The growth of neural circuits involved in social relationships thus decreases. As the brain is biased to perceiving threat, the traumatised child, who learns to associate eye contact with danger, will avoid it (Perry and Pollard, 1998). Without practice, the effort of sustaining eye contact becomes more painful, and the child's expectations of rejection are realised.

A case vignette in Chapter 6 illustrates how a child named "Pearl", who had been unable to recognise social signals, was taught these skills in play. But when the behaviour of children placed for adoption or long-term foster care is so anti-social that it leads to their being blamed or excluded from social groups, and to promised support from family and friends being withdrawn, their adoptive parents and foster carers can feel under huge pressure.

Raising maltreated children to be responsible and creative requires substitute parents to break the child's fixed patterns. Warner-Rogers and Reed (2008) advise that, in order to be able to treat these difficulties effectively, we need to understand the human brain. Our brains evolve to enable us to predict others' thoughts and this means that the fears of children who suffer perpetual anxiety are only assuaged when they are able to feel secure and be self-reflective.

Fortunately, given committed, loving relationships, we find that their brains are capable of "rewiring" and that an effective way to achieve this is via communicating through play, which provides a nurturing and sensory experience.

The senses

From the beginning of life, we experience the world through the five senses. Robinson (2001) reflects that sensory experience allows us to think visually, aurally, kinaesthetically, spatially, and in other ways well beyond conventional reasoning. Experiments on rats reveal that there is a "window" for the senses to develop. When the rats' eyes are covered during this sensitive period, they remain blind for life. Yet, while sight remains prominent in its value to our survival, sound is catching up.

Annaz *et al* (2008) observed that, even before they are born, babies recognise their mother's voice. In correlating children's sensitivity to sound patterns with their language skill, Kraus (2010) found that playing a musical instrument enhanced children's reading and listening skills. Soft lilting sounds soothe; harsh sounds, especially verbal abuse, can have negative and frightening effects (Teicher *et al*, 2006).

Severely traumatised children can be physiologically and emotionally alarmed by an unexpected touch, however well intentioned or innocently it occurs. This fear-induced sensitivity interferes with their ability to be in close relationships. The use of sensory substances that invite enjoyment and build tolerance of "safe touch" is described in Chapter 1.

Memory

"Working memory" requires the ability to recall knowledge that is relevant to resolving particular problems (Damasio, 2001) and capacity to sustain attention (Cowan *et al*, 2003). The prefrontal cortex, described by Jones *et al* (2004) as a "search engine" for retrieval of relevant information, is affected by the individual's perceptions, which are, of course, based on their experience.

On the outskirts of the pre-frontal cortex are significant, though tiny, insula and anterior cortices that co-ordinate thoughts and emotions with bodily experiences (Cozolino, 2006), which is why, when we feel impatient, we might become aware of, say, tapping our feet or drumming our fingers. These anterior insula cortices gather information and detect subtle patterns that we wouldn't otherwise notice. Lehrer (2009) explains that they are full of receptors for dopamine, a neurochemical that generates pleasurable feelings and helps us to regulate our emotions and make decisions. Yet these cortices also act to inhibit us from making the decisions we don't want to make, by activating avoidance mechanisms such as disgust. Since these cortices are particularly activated in novel or challenging situations (Todd and Lewis, 2008, p.292), they are surely integral to the creative processes.

Stimulating creativity

Treatises on neuroscience rarely mention creativity and past wisdom has led to a misguided belief that feelings get far too much in the way of rationality. Yet we need emotions in order to apply rationality. Teachers, for instance, rely on their instincts and emotions as a shortcut to making quick decisions in the process of organising groups of children or dealing with disputes. In fact, research on how the brain allows us to make successful decisions finds our emotions to be the determining influence (Lehrer, 2009). Therefore, the more we encourage children to explore their thoughts and feelings via the use of sensory stimuli, including stories, that evoke reactions from the emotional brain parts, the more their brains will be stimulated.

To be creative requires us to develop skills of perception and the capacity to reflect on the past in order to plan for the future. Developing this capacity is of particular importance for children who focus on the present and need help to think originally. Brown and Vaughan (2009) reflect that 'play lies at the core of creativity and innovation'. As soon as children start thinking and making the "un-thought" known, the strong links ("top down" pathways) between the frontal lobe and cerebellum enable other parts of the brain to co-ordinate more effectively.

To remember stories requires the use of both sides of the brain, although Cozolino (2006) observed young people to rely mainly on one side or the other. So let's explore how we can stimulate creative thinking and build self-esteem in those used to assuming that they are hopeless and helpless.

Howard-Jones et al (2008) discovered that creative artistic activity resulted in deeper reflective thinking, insight and sensitivity. After all, relaxing in play enables children to become more aware of gaze, facial expression, posture, touch and proximity, all of which are usually underlying conscious awareness. Fonagy et al (1996) and Main et al (1985) noted that meta-communication, skills such as the non-verbal signals used by secure children in play, enabled them to comment on their thinking, to reflect and to plan. Sherborne (1991) developed "push and pull" games that allow less able children to discover their strength and agility, and enhance their confidence.

Dramatic play

As well as Moreno's therapeutic use of drama, important influences include Brecht's "epic theatre" (Willett, 1977) in which actors break out of role and invite the audience to critically appraise what they see, so the spectator will 'no longer see characters on stage as unalterable, uninfluenceable, helplessly delivered over to their fate' (Goosens, 1997, p.6), but will realise that we act according to circumstances in which we find ourselves.

In dramatic play, as shown in Chapters 5 and 6, children gain a reflected view of themselves from others' perspectives that are different but related both to them and the role they play. The late dramatist, Augustus Boal, observed actors to operate at both real and surreal levels and unconsciously transfer onto the stage things from real life as 'the ghosts have a tendency to come back to their places and repeat the same things' (Boal, 1995, p.27). Drama's strength lies in its catalytic effect: 'It opens doors' (Grotowski, 1975).

A play is open to interpretation by its audience according to what they see being expressed. A key factor that distinguishes "drama" from "play" is its concentration on "role". The plays in Chapter 5 illustrate that the engagement of adoptive parents in a re-enactment of their children's history can help children achieve a sense of belonging and ownership in the new family. Robert Landy, dramatherapist, has argued that human beings are role takers and role players by nature, with the innate ability 'to imagine oneself as another and to act like another' (Landy, 2001, p.31).

In my experience, this ability cannot be assumed of emotionally deprived children who struggle to live with ambivalence and need help to achieve a balance, in order to be able to acknowledge their feelings while remaining in control of them. Jennings (2009) found severely neglected children unable to engage with any kind of imaginary role. Nevertheless, they can benefit from having someone give them insight and friendship to support their self-learning, as revealed by feedback from parents and children (see Chapter 7).

A primary aim of this work is, therefore, to encourage adoptive parents and foster carers to engage playfully with their children, and to enjoy stories and creative activities as a vehicle to resolving the children's emotional problems.

How the book is structured

Chapter 1 explains the purpose of creative activity and describes how to involve children in sensory and imaginary play. A step-by-step structure is provided for creating stories to address particular issues. Suggestions for settings of fantasy and reality are given, to encourage children to develop their own story. The metaphors used in play are discussed to help parents understand their significance and the meaning they can have for children.

The stories in **Chapter 2** illustrate a method for dealing with autobiographical material that respects children's need for privacy to work through difficult memories and cope with bewildering change. For example, the story of *The elephant who felt different* helps children to understand that when they panic, their brain is remembering the "unwanted" story, and now they can rewrite the episode as they would prefer it to have been. Each story is preceded by a case vignette and followed by discussion points and suggested activities.

Chapter 3 addresses specific predicaments such as feeling "different". For example, the story of *The elf who hated Christmas* helped a child adapt to foster care at a time of special emotional significance. When children who are well supported by their caregivers realise that their troublesome reactions stem from circumstances for which they are not to blame, they can learn to trust and manage their impulses.

Chapter 4 explores the use of traditional and modern stories such as *Aladdin* and *The Wizard of Oz*. The stories are supported by creative activities in order to invite exploration of feelings that assist recovery from earlier trauma. From the courage of fictional heroes, children gain hope for their own future.

Chapter 5 describes and illustrates the involvement of adoptive and foster families in re-enacting brief plays of their children's histories. The merits of script and improvisation are discussed and a structure proposed for preparation, performance, and processing the feelings that emerge. Sample scripts draw on children's experience of past abuse, fuelled by parents' relational problems, often exacerbated by illness, learning difficulties and substance misuse.

Chapter 6 focuses on using the safety of metaphor and fantasy contexts, within which children can replay aspects of their life history. The application of "role" and employment of everyday settings is illustrated for the purpose of addressing issues of social ineptness and poor hygiene that stem from early neglect and abuse. In play, children practise ways to "be" with people, and from this, they learn to accommodate their new parents' expectations.

Chapter 7 describes the progress made by the children and families who have engaged in this work. The first part illustrates narratives created by children. Case examples illustrate the preferred ways to manage conflict and rivalry, learning from which heightened children's self-esteem. The second part aims to help parents track their children's development. A template is provided to measure children's creativity and social skills. The author reflects on the impact on children and parents of their engagement in this "Theatre of Attachment" model of creative dramatic play and storytelling.

In conclusion, change can come through storymaking, which can help to enhance children's "meta-communication" skills. Identifying with the experience of fictional characters inspires children to challenge their long-held assumptions built on past internalisation of shame and to work towards more satisfactory resolution. Healing relationships alter the balance of the brain's networks and in so doing, alleviate anxiety. Stories with "happy endings" invite demoralised children to strive for a hopeful future that incorporates a valued relationship with and attachment to a person or family who can love and protect them.

There is an appendix: *Guide to empathic communication*

Storytelling

1

This chapter describes how to use creative approaches to help children attach to substitute parents. The first part discusses the value of storymaking and its role in resolving difficulties that impede attachment, and describes how the use of sensory materials can stimulate children to create their own stories. The second part guides parents in supporting the play and explains the symbolic meanings and metaphors that children use; while the third part focuses on processes in play and ways to communicate with fearful children who challenge the boundaries.

Creating stories for children

The art of creating stories can be learned. As so many parents rely on the media to entertain and educate children, and perhaps are unaccustomed to play or shy of "getting it wrong", the following exercise shows how easy it is to tell a story about events that have had an emotional impact.

- Write the story of what happened when you went to work today.

- Tell a story about some gossip or news exchanged in the last conversation that you had with a close friend or relative.

- Describe a dramatic or surprising event that you witnessed.

- Write your memory of a family event recalled differently by others.

- Describe a time when you were called upon to help someone.

Most children will develop their own narrative, especially when they are given access to materials they can use in an imaginative and individual way. If they lack confidence in play, an easy way to invite their engagement is to tell them a story. Stories with a therapeutic purpose are given a setting that lends a necessary distance and aims to illustrate feelings to which children can relate.

Cozolino (2006) explains that narratives build new connections between brain cells, and that these reinforce "cause and effect" thinking through the characters in the story showing readers how to get by. When children hear stories that have meaning for them, they will unconsciously make a connection to their own experience.

Stories also offer a sense of safety – the story, after all, is about something that happens to someone else – compared with drama, which, because of its immediacy and one's own role within it, can be more exposing and threatening. Storytelling provides a framework for families to enjoy quality time together by encouraging spontaneity and inviting emotional connection.

Magic and transformation

"Magic" has the dual advantage of engendering fun as well as stimulating the imagination, until the child develops a more sophisticated means of resolution. In stories, anything can happen...so magic can be deployed to bring about change and enact a transformation in a person's fortune and circumstances, thus demonstrating a way forward that conveys a sense of hope. In creating and dramatising their story, children discover that the skills involved in resolving matters fictionally can be transferred to resolving problems in real life. However, before their emotional problems can be addressed, the more traumatised children, who react fearfully to textures or being touched, may need sensory play that helps them to tolerate physical contact.

Using sensory materials

Children who have very limited experience of play are often bewildered by choice and do not know how to use creative materials. Traditionally, play therapy settings have provided a wide variety of toys and materials, but this presumes that the child is able to exercise choice and knows how to engage in play, experience of which the most neglected children lack. Perry (2009) has developed a "neurosequential model of therapeutics" (NMT) based on the history and current functioning of children subjected to parental drug and alcohol misuse pre-birth, and abuse during their early years when the brain is developing most rapidly. His model replicates the normal sequence of brain development (i.e. from the base upwards). Children are given repetitive (daily) sensory input of music, movement and massage to help them regulate the damaged regions of the lower brain. Connections can then be rebuilt with the higher regions, thus enabling the child to develop in satisfactory relationship with others.

The physical and emotional components of sensory materials can stimulate as well as soothe children who are anxious about play or who fear touch. For example, shaving foam mixed with cornflour and water makes snowy "mountains" to which a sprinkling of paprika can create a "volcano" that "erupts" on adding bicarbonate of soda. Given individual attention, children rarely require structure and their resulting action or play often presents a "story". Even adolescents enjoy this activity, once they understand that stories have been the means by which we humans have been entertained and educated through the centuries. Furthermore, as Cozolino (2006) explains, storytelling helps our brains to work more efficiently.

Given encouragement and support to experiment with a variety of creative materials, for example, sand, clay, paint, puppets, dolls and other toys, children like Luke, aged 11, become open to the idea that life can change for the better. Although adopted in infancy, his pre-birth exposure to alcohol seemed to be the most likely cause of his struggle to keep up with his peers in mainstream school. Often bullied, Luke used food to assuage his anxiety; however, projective play helped him to understand his needs.

. . . .

CASE EXAMPLE: **LUKE**

In play with puppets, Luke constructed a tale of Olympic-style games in which competitors realised that to ensure success they must utilise their skills. Tiger's advice to 'Just believe in yourself' gave his friend, Moose, the necessary confidence to beat his opponent. Luke, in role as "Moose", explained that being confident enabled him to listen to advice, focus on the task, use his special talents and all his strength and to plan his timing carefully. In the final event, a competition to see who could make people laugh the most, Penguin used his ingenuity to outsmart Monkey, by tickling him!

Luke's imagination was particularly fired by dramatic play, which gave him the affirmation he needed to manage his anxiety. In another of his stories, he transformed an "evil genius" into a "kindly magician" who rendered a scary "vampire" helpless. Feeling free to explore his inner self, Luke, to use his own phrase, learned to 'fly without being scared of heights'. Joining and participating in a dance–drama group further enhanced his confidence.

. . . .

The importance of fictional distance

Neglected children often need help to name feelings and may struggle to distinguish between the "real" and "unreal". Early abuse leads to emotions being shut down and the child who ceases to recognise his own feelings or those of others may view another child as an object, like a doll, incapable of feeling. For children who have been locked in their room and assaulted, life has been so terrifying that a "real" setting can re-ignite traumatic memories. Cattanach (1999) advises the use of a play mat to demarcate the "play space" from the "non playing space", in order to maintain the necessary "distance".

Using fantasy

Stories set in fantasy give the protection of being unreal. In identifying with a hero in a difficulty similar to their own, and seeing matters resolved in the story, children derive hope for their own future. In the course of acting out the story, a child can allow "rescue" and try out the heroic qualities that he would not view as realistic in the context of his own life.

Younger children are usually more comfortable with fantasy and instinctively guide receptive adults to fictional contexts that allow them to process their feelings.

· ·

CASE EXAMPLE: **JASON**

Five-year-old Jason's parents had committed suicide. He processed his loss by killing dragons and extinguishing fires in the dramas that he created. These fantasies allowed him to explore his painful feelings in parallel with, but separate from, his actual experience. In the play, he gained control over his sense of perpetual uncertainty.

· ·

In fantasy play, action can take place in outer space, in castles, jungles, oceans, or forests populated with all manner of aliens, princesses, giants, animals, mermaids, elves and fairies. Battles may be fought between pirates, or Robin Hood and the Sheriff, or between children and monsters. Dinosaurs are symbols of the past and aeroplanes facilitate escape. Deserts, reminiscent of thirst and emptiness, can be the setting for a "magic carpet ride" to an oasis, a place of plenty (see box on facing page). Children learn that if change can occur in stories, it may happen in real life, by applying similar problem-solving techniques of using their imagination, and asking for the help of friends.

Using real-life scenarios

Children who are older and/or who lack confidence in applying imagination may initially be more comfortable with the familiar real-life scenarios of "shopping", "hospitals", "school", "police stations" or "car racing tracks". These scenes may gradually evolve as a fantasy in the process of exploring complex feelings (see examples in Chapters 4 and 6). If a child develops a drama based on "real life", it remains important to retain their privacy by deeming it fictional, since to directly reflect on its resemblance to the child's actual experience may prompt a defensive reaction.

FANTASY SETTINGS FOR STORYMAKING

Castles occupied by kings and queens, knights, handmaidens, jesters

Oceans with mermaids, sharks, whales, an octopus stuck in coral, pirate ships sailing through storms, visiting tropical as well as barren islands

Deserts with camels, sand dunes, magic carpets, sand storms

Farms or woodland with animals that can speak

Fairy stories in which characters journey to unexpected places

Aeroplane hijacks in which heroes and heroines rescue the passengers

Battle scenes from history or set in the future – good versus evil, star wars, intergalactic superpowers

Stories about impending disaster in which the hero protects the citizens of Earth

Dinosaurs – carnivores, vegetarians – in a battle for survival

Jungles where wild animals roam but who are under threat of urban development – who wins?

Circus with a clown who can't laugh, lions that roar, trapeze artistes who fall

Steps to storymaking

A simple story structure has a beginning, middle and end. The following structure is my adaptation of the six-part technique devised by Lahad (2000); pictures from magazines or the internet can provide inspiration to help children represent each part of their story.

- **The main character:** From observing the child's preferences and inclinations, choose a central character to which she will connect or that reminds you of the child. It might be an animal, bird, insect, sea creature, flower, elf, clown or witch. Dogs, cats and horses are very popular.

- **Support:** The main character will need a friend for support. It might be the same or different type of species, for instance, a flower could befriend a bumblebee or a horse could befriend a young boy.

- **Adventure or mission:** The "main character" will have a mission or a journey in the course of which a problem, obstacle or dilemma will be resolved. Choose a setting that will be appropriate for the action; an alternative time or place lends distance from real life. Decide on the season, weather and temperature in the story.

- **Problem:** Notice how the child makes you feel. This will guide you to how he may be feeling. Then think of a metaphor to illustrate the feeling, for example, crushed like a flower, confused as if "in a fog". You could think of several challenges for the main character to work through.

- **How the problem is overcome:** The friend can help the main character in her mission by imaginative, magical or realistic means.

- **How it turns out:** Consider the gains for the main character from having resolved the problem. What impact will it have? Does it bring about a transformation? Will it prompt him to seek support in future? Does it bring hope?

REAL-LIFE SETTINGS FOR STORYMAKING

Hospital, doctor's surgery, doctor/nurse, and patient

School – incidents in the playground and classroom

House moves – removal van – impact of change

Supermarket – food, clothes, toys, customers

Railway station/airport/taxi rank/bus stop – journeys – where to? Car race track accident – what happens?

Sports events – who gets the prize and why?

Park, picnic, unusual food, game of hide and seek, someone gets lost and scared

Birthday party or festive occasion – sharing food, warm wishes and gifts

Outings, day trips, theme parks, seaside

Steps to involving children in creative activity

Creative play can include clay, play dough, paint, sand and junk modelling. Providing one creative activity at a time avoids overwhelming a child. A small tray (available from pet shops) can be half filled with sand to provide sensory stimulus while toy people, animals, houses, cars, helicopters, trains and fences invite engagement in storytelling. While this option may appear to be limited, there are, in fact, several ways in which children might play with such a sand tray:

- Running the sand through their fingers, burying their hands, adding water to build sandcastles or hills, making a road, and so on.

- Hiding toys in the sand then inviting the parent to find them and vice versa – hide and seek play relates to the stage of learning "trust versus mistrust" (Erikson, 1963) and helps recovery of nurture and fun.

- Selecting toys to create tableaux in the sand tray from which action might follow and a story may spontaneously develop.

- Some children dislike the texture of sand and prefer to play with just the toys.

Advance preparation

- Choose a story that you know the child likes and may respond to.

- To complement the story, plan an activity that he or she will enjoy, such as painting or modelling (see Chapters 2, 3 and 4 for ideas).

- Ensure that you have all the materials and protective equipment necessary, in order to minimise the effort of clearing up later.

- Dispensing materials into small containers helps to avoid waste.

Playing with the child

Spread plastic sheets or newspapers on the floor if planning to use messy materials like water, sand, paint, collage and/or clay.

Read the story you have chosen from this book with the child. See the discussion points provided after the story for guidance on how to keep to the metaphor as much as possible without making a link to the child's own experience that might embarrass them.

Choose from some of the following play options, but set a time limit of 30 minutes if the child is under six or an hour for children over six years, as any longer can be too tiring and their interest may wane.

- Encourage the child to act out the story as heard, or to enact their version in the way they choose. In this pretend play, dressing-up clothes and props such as hats and bags help to distinguish the "role" from the actor, thus preserving the distance of it being a story.

- Begin a creative activity. Figures and scenery can be sculpted in play dough or clay, or in collages or painted, then various parts made into a story. Story cards or pictures from magazines can inspire ideas.

- During the course of painting a picture, modelling, etc. note the characteristics and emerging themes. Invite the child to tell a story. Tell the child you will write it for them as they tell the story.

- If the child is reluctant to tell a story, ask for their permission for you to create a story for them, based on what you observe in their paintings or models.

- You can do the same when playing with dolls' houses or cars. The vehicles can be given "personalities" and the story can be told from weaving together the events being played out on a mat.

- As you tell or listen to the story, comment on the feelings you notice, keeping to the fictional context. If the child struggles to find an outcome, you could suggest possibilities to choose from.

Allow a pessimistic outcome if that is the child's choice, but should it persist, comment that if everything in the world was bad, there would be no kind parents to cook nice dinners, no comfy beds to sleep in, or fun things to do. Suggest that creating stories that have a good ending is practice for real life.

Make a record of the story and read it to the child, then read it again at the start of the next time you play together, to remind them of their creative skills and what they were able to do. Children are usually more than willing to co-operate, delighted by adults' expressed interest in them. Seeing their stories recorded and (ideally) illustrated enhances their self-esteem and reinforces learning from having constructed solutions to their characters' difficulties.

Practical considerations

Children who have not had enough practice at play may show poor understanding of the medium. For example, they might mix all the paint colours together and then not transfer the paint to paper, or might pile it on until it drips over the edge, or use up all the glitter and sequins available to them.

Invite the child to enjoy mixing and stirring (less costly) flour and water, perhaps adding a few drops of food colouring (but beware of staining).

Using messy materials in play requires planning and this kind of play can be exhausting, but it does pay dividends. Children who play creatively make huge gains, both practically and emotionally, from permission to experiment as well as enjoying their parent's participation. As a result, they will learn more quickly to occupy themselves without the need for such close adult supervision.

Some children insist on being in control and may not co-operate if their parent tries to insist on creating stories or even just writing them down. Play needs to be voluntary and the child will gain more if parents join in, or remain present, rather than engage in a battle of wills.

Supporting the play

The longer children play, the more explicitly they reveal their thoughts and worries, so parents are advised to wait patiently rather than ask questions that a child may be unwilling or unable to answer. However, the play can invite dialogue about what is going on. The phrases suggested below can help you seek clarification in a way that conveys enthusiasm and deepening interest. You may sometimes "wonder" aloud what is happening without directly asking, and not mind if, or how soon, the child answers, for example, 'I see Power Ranger keeps blowing those houses up'. Wait for the child's response before asking for a reason. You might ask, 'Can I be on his team?' or 'Shall I be one of these guys?' letting the child direct his play in which he may give you a part.

While we aim for integration so that children will come to accept a balance of "good" and "bad" in people, including themselves, it remains important to communicate at the child's level. Young (pre-school age) and emotionally delayed children, who are still at the stage of "magical thinking", tend to perceive people in terms of "good" or "bad" (See Corrigan and Moore, 2011). To these young children, the parent might say: 'I'm trying to see who the "goodies" are'. If the child points to some figures, show curiosity and ask, 'OK, so which ones are the "baddies"?'

Here are some more examples:

'That looks scary! I wonder if anyone can help. Is this one nice or nasty?'

'Are there other ways she can rescue or help? Do we need a doctor?'

'Can any of these people help themselves? I wonder how/why not?'

'Is no one allowed to make mistakes? No? That's tough!'

'I wonder what might make things better for these guys?'

'Oh! I see he's the only one left alive! That's so sad! Who's going to cook his dinner? Suppose he gets hurt? He'll need some help to get better!'

If the child insists that 'No one can help', suggest the hero might like to have a friend to play with or a mum to give him a present on his birthday.

Facilitating children's problem-solving capacity

Once children have seen problems resolved fictionally, their interest is aroused in playing out their own stories. By engaging them in imaginative play and expressing a sincere interest in their thoughts, feelings, hopes, dreams, ambitions and the choices they make, parents encourage children to discover new possibilities. Creative play leads to improved relationships between children and parents and, in the long term, aids psychological health (Russ, 2004). Cozolino (2006) advises that children need to discover for themselves how the world works and form their own conclusions. Therefore, in this form of creative play, parents are encouraged to listen, reflect, join in and offer suggestions when invited.

Children from violent homes are likely to play out catastrophic scenes and to view positive outcomes as unrealistic. Until they are ready to allow "rescue", it is generally best to acknowledge their feelings of hopelessness and despair. Some will have learned to repress feelings in order to protect themselves. They may idealise their past, refuting any evidence to the contrary. Yet, in the course of play in which conflicting memories are explored, children will gradually compare the different ways they have been treated. Their new parents' continuing interest in them will help them to trust and make new attachments.

However, children will test out their parents' availability in play situations, and the third part of this chapter describes how to maintain safe boundaries to ensure that play can be enjoyable for both children and participating adults.

The search for meaning in children's play

Once this creative process is underway, parents will want to interpret the meaning of their child's play. What does the action symbolise? What significance does it have? Children hope that the adult will understand what they are trying to show them without having to spell it out.

Some abused children may be too scared to articulate their fear, especially if, in the past, they were threatened with extreme penalty, should they "tell". Others may unconsciously process memories but not have the words to describe or explain them. To one child, the police can be a threat, to another, a source of rescue. Magic can symbolise disenchantment and chaos, or can facilitate exciting and desired transformations. In sand, toys may be buried for a multitude of reasons, including putting characters to "bed" or in a safe place, disposing of an unwanted threat, tidying up, or simply playing a game of "hide and seek".

By noticing the repetition of children's phrases and actions, you will be able to identify their preoccupations (See Chapters 4 and 7). One child may bash her dolls to punish them for the way she has been treated; another will enact war scenes reminiscent of violence that he witnessed. A key part of helping children to recognise emotional cues is to name feelings. The metaphors that arise in their play can often help us guess at what has happened to them. Overleaf is a selection of the kind of metaphors that are commonly used by children to represent their experience, in order to enable parents to create stories that address their child's damaging self-perceptions and fears.

The child's feelings	Metaphors and symbols
Isolated, disempowered	Locked in prison or dungeon
Terror, anticipating menace	Crocodiles, sharks, piranhas
Disintegrated, shocked	Bombs, grenades
Constantly pressured to perform	Being stuck in a swamp
Conflict (domestic)	War, storms, disasters
Crushed, despair	Avalanche, drowning in floods
Confusion, uncertainty, obscurity	Smoke, fog, sand storm, darkness
Overwhelmed, devastated	Tornado, earthquake, tsunami
Shrinking, unseen, insignificant	Burial, camouflage, insects
Abused, disgust, repulsion	Snakes, fish, slime, stink bombs
Deceived, betrayed, tricked	Witch, evil spells, masquerade
Frozen, unfeeling	North Pole, Snow Queen
Exhaustion	Burial, sleep
Feeling "different"	Aliens
Hope, desire	Rainbow, prince/princess, gold
Order, control, new perspectives	Police, helicopters, aeroplanes
Enlightenment	Light, apocalypse, a "vision"
Desire for comfort	Food
Trust, belief in change	Magic, happy endings

Maintaining safe boundaries

Fearful children who are unused to parental guidance can appear intent on trying to sabotage their parent's best intentions. It is frightening for children to feel out of control of their strong feelings. Unforeseen triggers can cause them to regress to the infantile stage of needing a parent to contain these feelings for them. Play offers a wonderful opportunity for children to be in charge but difficulties can arise if they have not learned to respect boundaries.

Setting limits in boisterous play

The clearest rules to establish are: no hitting or throwing, no hurting of self or others, and no (deliberate) damage to property. That said, boys, especially, love tickling and play-fighting and often struggle with limits. It is important to agree in advance that tickling stops if either of you want it to, and to establish on which parts of the body it is allowed, such as elbows, knees and ankles.

Play-fighting, with plastic swords, for example, teaches body awareness. Fake injuries can be conveyed by agreed signals so that no one is hurt. However, if after two warnings, the child continues to get "carried away", you should explain firmly, but sympathetically : 'I can see you have not understood the rules about safety. We'll try again another day, when you can keep to the rules.'

Acknowledging feelings

Some children rely on coercion as their modus operandi for survival, so will try to exert control by demanding that parents be flexible and give in to them. For example, Corrie, aged six, acting as "parent", insisted on another sweet on the pretext that 'We are playing pretend and I'm the mum so I'm allowed!' By acknowledging her strong desire – 'I know you want those sweets' – her mother displayed empathy for her feelings. She then reasserted the house rule: 'You can eat the sweets after tea'.

An alternative strategy is for the parent to step out of their fictional role to ask the child: 'If you were a sensible parent, what would you do? What should mothers do to prevent their child taking more than their fair share or becoming ill from too many sweets?' If the child continues not to co-operate, stop the play, put the sweets away and promise that you will play another time.

Modelling

Children love to experiment with power but it can be daunting for parents to be cast in role as the "child". Yet, taking this role offers a valuable opportunity to model the child's feelings and show how vulnerable you suspect she feels. The parent can acknowledge feeling powerless: 'I'm not finding this easy! I wish I knew what to do!' Acting as "Snow White", sent by the seven dwarves to another home, you can own to feeling scared that your new mum will turn out to be evil like the queen. In their fictional role, a parent may comment that children need adults to be kind, helpful, and protective, and to set an example, explain things, and so on, to model nurturing attitudes. The parent can also express their child's desires. By acting as child, you could say, 'I wish we could go on a holiday! Where would you take me?' Within this fictional context, the "parent" (child) can plan a treat or activity, and the child thereby practises negotiating from a parental perspective.

Rehearsing expression of feelings

Children may reveal overwhelming and catastrophic experiences through play that they otherwise could not express in words. Rachel, aged 11, was in foster care. Her play featured a monster whose destructive acts were a projection of her memories of domestic violence. She then made a shift from fantasy to drama that was far closer to reality (evident in her files), showing remarkable courage in doing so. Rachel cast the therapist as mother and herself as baby. In the play, she revealed experience of abuse and abandonment by directing the "mother" to be cruelly sadistic to her "baby". Having agreed that no one would be hurt during play, she rehearsed "punching". Later, when the "child" ran away from home, Rachel considered how it should have been (see overleaf).

. . . .

CASE EXAMPLE: **RACHEL**

The play began with the mother angrily ramming a bottle in the crying baby's mouth. The baby was scalded and punished for crawling away. Rachel directed the mother to (pretend to) spank her and push her away. When, as the growing child, she wandered off, her mother only pretended to look for her, wishing to protect herself from trouble with social workers. At age five, the child had bad dreams. Desolate, she ran away from home but the mother always found her and punished her. Defending against painful early memories, Rachel insisted this was 'just a story'.

. . . .

Rachel may have been using the "mother" to project anger that she felt most strongly towards her father, who had sexually abused her for years. In her plays, a character representing "Dad" was consistently and irredeemably irresponsible, and lacked conscience. Rachel could not verbalise her confused feelings, especially that she had affection for him. This posed another challenge – how to authentically portray the character's abusive behaviour without ignoring his positive qualities? It is important to try to explore the whole person, rather than focus on aspects that are either solely negative or overly idealised.

Inviting the child's advice

Fantasy play can be a useful vehicle for parents who are trying to encourage children to become self-aware of their knowledge and understanding. The parent might volunteer for the role of "junior witch" and say, 'I wish I was as smart as you! I got thrown out of witch school. My spells were useless – the teachers said I didn't follow the rules. I wonder what I must do to be allowed back?' Children appreciate being asked for advice and often find they know what advice to give. Alternatively, in a theatrical aside, the parent might say, 'I feel like being naughty though I know it won't help me in the long run! What should I do?' In this way, you acknowledge the child's mixed up feelings but invite helpful responses, empowering them to develop their own social skills.

Encouraging trust

Children who have always felt unwanted may cast their (new) parent in the role of a cruel character, revealing that they expect denigration, consistent with their former experience. Although it is important to respect the child's request, the parent may become increasingly half-hearted in role as "witch", at being as "cruel" as the child expects, by making theatrical asides to convey their discomfort: 'This is tricky. It's boring being bad! Can I have a go at your role?' Afterwards, the parent might say, 'I'm glad you showed me how badly you've been hurt. I want you to feel safe with me. I'm going to take the best possible care of you!'

However much substitute parents feel rejected, their grieving children need them to show genuine concern. The role of "Prince Charming" or "Fairy Godmother" gives you the opportunity to explain: 'It's my job to look after you. I love you/care about you and want you to be safe and well.' In time, with consistency of care, children will believe you. Meanwhile, in play, the child can experiment with the possibility of such assertions proving true.

Coping with frustration

All children can be rude at times. Frustration can prompt some to use the fictional "role" to denigrate and undermine parents. This is a strategy of self-protection developed by children who experience the world as a hostile place. They may have been betrayed and blamed by adults who failed to explain the reasons for their actions.

Daniel, aged nine, blamed himself for his maltreatment but dispelled his intense feeling by projecting it onto someone else. In dramatic play, his adoptive mother, cast in role as "king's servant", responded by saying, 'It's hard for me when you are so rude!' She allowed him time to adjust, but if his abusive attitude continued, she would say, 'I'm tired! What shall we do next?' Daniel usually reeled off a string of complaints about being taken to places he didn't want to go and not being listened to. His mother explained that everyone feels cross at times and that we all have to do things we don't like. Talking about what makes a person feel happy or scared distracted him and enabled her to offer a different activity, as one might to a younger child.

If non-verbal signals, for example, the child's manner or voice, indicate that they are acting as (and therefore feeling like) a child far younger than their chronological age, it is often more helpful to distract them out of a confrontation so as to prevent an escalation that is likely to leave them stuck. Praising them for things they have got right encourages success. Affection and approval given in the context of "make believe" is more tolerable for wary children. Although play with traumatised children can be exhausting, it reaps rewards far sooner than by relying solely on verbal communication as a means to resolve misunderstandings.

Exploring worries

Children who have not learned empathy can become argumentative. The appendix gives examples of empathic responses to a range of situations that commonly arise. Used with care, role reversal can also help to resolve conflict likely to arise over, for instance, how late the child goes to bed, how far they can ride their bike, or which friend is allowed home to play. In role, say, as "teacher and pupil", each can guess at the other's thoughts as a way to navigate towards a mutually acceptable compromise. Psychologist Daniel Hughes draws from dramatherapy methods to ask the child, 'Can I be you for a minute?' Then, speaking as the child, he describes the thoughts and fears that he believes are going on inside the child's head and checks if he is correct. Undertaken sensitively, this method is most effective. In dramatic play I have employed a technique that works similarly.

. . . .

CASE EXAMPLE

A girl of 12 acted as a thief who (like her birth father) continually outwitted authority. The therapist, cast in role as "police officer", stood outside a cupboard in which the thief was hiding and reflected on her worries for the shopkeeper (victim), who was losing her business, herself (in trouble for not making an arrest), and the thief (as to how far he might go, if the police didn't catch him). This prompted the girl to step out of the cupboard and decide that the culprit had to be caught, the role play having given her a moral compass.

. . . .

Personifying problems

The consequences of neglect and trauma can cause children acute embarrassment and make them feel powerless to alter unwelcome behaviour perceived to be "weird", abnormal or problematic. Contextualising such behaviour (by explaining its source) helps to "normalise" the child's predicament. Selekman (2005) proposes that, in order to avoid shame and blame, it is helpful to separate undesired behaviour from the child by personifying it, giving it a name such as "Attitude", "Rage" or "Jealousy", and noticing the child or young person's efforts to deal with their problem, saying, for example, 'Poor Attitude! I bet he's really annoying you today! Let's see if we can make him feel better!' The young person can be invited to think of an acceptable compromise and the family encouraged to work towards a mutually satisfactory arrangement.

Traumatised children find it hard to take pleasure in life, so may armour themselves against anticipated disapproval by finding fault, as a means of protecting themselves from anticipated rejection. To help them learn how to enjoy life, parents can remind them of pleasures such as being out in sunny weather, playing in snow, laughing, or eating their favourite foods. Rewarding experiences stimulate the "happy chemicals" in the brain that insulate against the damaging effects of fear and anxiety, thereby enabling self-regulation. Below is a list of suggested rewarding activities that can encourage bonding with a child.

- Sharing stories
- Telling jokes
- Hand lotion massage
- Singing and dancing together
- Play "Stack of Hands"
- Cooking, baking cakes
- Feeding child in your arms
- Blowing and catching bubbles
- Swimming and cycle rides
- Infant games, e.g. "Incy wincy spider", "This little piggy"

- Playing cards or dominoes
- Clapping games
- Inventing handshakes
- Looking through photo albums
- Doing household jobs together
- Watching movies together
- Playing with a pet together
- Drawing pictures of shared feelings
- Giving reassurance: 'You are staying here!'
- Planning for tomorrow

"Claiming"

In delivering a story, use of the third person narrative (s/he) is recommended as some children can find the emotional intensity of "you" too overwhelming.

Soft, soothing music can set the atmosphere for a story that begins with the moment of birth. The child (provided she is willing) is held by the parent in a soft warm fleecy blanket, given a baby bottle (with milk or water) or a warm drink, and baby toys. The parent comments on the child's endearing features, for example, their eyes or the soft curve of their cheeks, and describes how he/she would play with her if she was their baby. Lacher *et al* (2005) found that such narratives have enabled parents to see their child with fresh eyes. I have found it equally effective in reassuring the child about their now belonging to a new family. Parents can help children feel they belong by telling and retelling these stories, looking at different periods of their childhood, and reassuring them that in this family, they will be staying, no matter what.

2

Life histories – using stories to explore, reflect and understand

This chapter illustrates how stories that parallel children's experiences can help abused children in a sensitive way to explore feelings about, and gain understanding of, past experiences that are often far more horrifying than many adults can bear to imagine. The stories are a means of resolving difficulties that impede children's progress in forming secure relationships with those caring for them.

The purpose of autobiographical work

The importance for children in care to understand their life history has been long established by leading experts in the neuroscience of child development (Siegel, 1999; Perry and Szalavitz, 2006) and the psychology of child abuse and trauma (Balbernie and Glazer, 2001). The most common practice in life story work is to produce a book that tells the child's story, describes their background and origins, and explains what happened and why decisions were taken to separate them from their birth family. But babies and young children, being too young to understand these explanations, may continue to feel abandoned and worthless. Some worry that they may have been kidnapped and may fantasise that if only their birth family knew where they lived, they could return to live with them. Even when children have been given explanations, many may not have made full sense of why they are in substitute care and blame themselves for it.

Some children dread the shaming nature of the explanation for why they came into care, and so feel reluctant to engage with it. Sharing a child's history with them is a delicate business, ideally one to be undertaken by trained professionals who are supervised. As many families do not have access to this kind of support, I would encourage adoptive parents and foster carers to try a narrative approach to help their children to come to terms with what has happened to them. However, it is recommended that parents discuss the resultant feelings that this can arouse with someone whom they trust to understand and empathise with both them and their child.

The safest way to begin this process is by reading a story that parallels the child's experience. Most children prefer the privacy of fiction to factual accounts of their history because the former allows them to accept or reject any connection to their own lives. A story that projects the central character as a brave, heroic survivor is a means to show that no one invites or deserves adversity, and helps to relieve children of self-blame for situations beyond their control. Yet blaming their birth parents can place the child in a further quandary as the child may reason, 'Since my parent is violent (or mentally ill), I'll probably turn out to be the same!'

The stories presented here show that we cannot help being affected by our experience. They illustrate how events combine to make it harder for the main character's birth parents to give their offspring the care and protection they need. The stories convey that an improved quality of care can lead to a more promising future. As children realise that the intention is to celebrate their survival, they may begin to ask questions about their history. At that stage, if and when the child wants to share their memories and hear more about what happened to them, parents can offer the facts in language appropriate to their age and understanding (Corrigan and Moore, 2011).

When children's recollections differ from the "official account", parents can explain that the written information came from people who knew only what they saw and heard, and that people often recall events differently, so some details may be incomplete or not completely accurate. Adding children's memories to the "official account" will help them to feel validated.

Stories as metaphors for adversity

The stories below will help children to make connections with and explore their earlier experiences. It is important to choose the story carefully and vital to obtain as much background information as possible to avoid shaming or shocking already traumatised children. For example, it is all too easy to make wrong assumptions, such as assuming that a home had been squalid, when in fact the parent had been too obsessed with hygiene to allow the child to play. Adopters and foster carers need to be cautious to avoid suggesting, either literally or by implication, anything that may have occurred, without sufficient evidence to support their assumptions.

To guard against this risk, the stories are set in imaginative contexts, with animals or flowers often used to represent the "child", as a way to retrieve memories from real life; it helps to find out which animals, plant, or other "character" the chid may feel a connection to. After hearing the story, the child can choose an activity. Parents are advised to join in play but should allow the child to lead (see Chapter 1 for guidance).

The stories below were created for children presenting with particular issues. Brief summaries of the reasons for referral, the child's history and the main themes of the story are followed by the story itself. Some discussion points are suggested along with a simple activity to engage the child.

FEELING "DIFFERENT"

Reason for referral
Joel, aged seven, had been placed for adoption. In his new school, he felt "different" to the other children, who resented him trying to control them.

History
Joel's birth mother had disappeared, leaving him to fend for himself. He had had to eat potato peelings from dustbins in order to survive.

The story
A young, abandoned elephant called Hercules is persuaded to follow a kind man home, where his wife welcomes and cares well for him. At his new home, Hercules is unfamiliar with the toilet and struggles to make his needs and worries understood. At school, he finds his prior experiences do not match those of his peers and he feels embarrassed to write about his life. He craves to fit in but assumes that, by trumpeting louder, he can make others listen. His skewed memory makes it harder to meet expectations; then being taken to live in a zoo feels like yet another rejection.

Outcome
Joel experienced the move to his "keeping family" as a bit like being in a zoo, with lots of people coming to look at him. He lost the freedom he had been used to in his early years of living without boundaries. Yet, like the young elephant in the story, Joel found that when someone listened to him, life took a turn for the better, and this helped him settle into his new school.

The elephant who felt different

Once upon a time, there was a young elephant called Hercules. When he was very young, his mummy wandered off and left him. Hercules had no idea where she was. He looked for her all over the place but couldn't find her anywhere. Tired out, Hercules sat down and cried! He had never felt so lonely and scared in his life. He was hungry. The scraps lying around didn't taste right but Hercules ate them to stay alive even though they made him feel sick!

A passerby saw Hercules crying. He asked what was wrong. Hercules tried to explain that he was looking for his mum but the man didn't understand him. Still, he was a kind man so he beckoned, saying, 'Tell you what, you can come and stay in my house!' Hercules was so relieved to hear a kind voice…he plodded along, following the man to his house. The man's wife was very welcoming and made up a bed for Hercules. She showed him where the toilet was and cooked him a pan of delicious stew. Hercules ate it all up! That night he had a really good long sleep, as he was soooo tired!

At first, Hercules was happy in his new home, even though it was a bit tricky for a young elephant to work out what to do about the strange toilet that was designed for an entirely different creature! But elephants are very intelligent so Hercules was able to figure out a way of using the toilet that kept him out of bother.

The man and his wife told Hercules that now that he was living in their house, he'd better start going to the local school. Being a smart kind of guy, Hercules was keen to learn but suppressed a sigh of dread as he wondered how he was going to get on with these new sorts of creatures he wasn't used to and who weren't used to him. School seemed OK at first. Everyone moved up to make room for Hercules to perch at his desk. The trouble started when the teacher asked him questions he didn't know how to answer. Then she told the class to write stories about their life! Hercules knew she would never understand how hard this was for him because, for one thing, she didn't know how upsetting it was for your mum to wander off like that leaving you to live with strangers. Hercules wanted to write stories like the others and be like them, but he hadn't lived their life, so he couldn't work out what to say!

In the playground Hercules wanted to join in with the children, but when he trumpeted, they only heard loud noises and didn't realise he wanted to play with them. Hercules trumpeted louder. Foam came out of his trunk, spraying everyone. The children got scared and Hercules only got more and more cross.

As time went on, Hercules continued to enjoy the food at the man and lady's house, so of course he grew bigger and bigger and bigger! Soon, it seemed that whichever way he stretched his trunk or flapped his ears to listen to anything interesting, he'd knock over an ornament or crash into something. The man and the lady told him off, forgetting how big elephants grow. (Well, elephants can't help that, can they?) Hercules tried to explain but they didn't understand him.

They consulted their friends, and then put an advert in the newspaper to ask if anyone with a really big house could look after Hercules while he was still growing. Someone advised them that elephants really need to live with their own kind and suggested a zoo.

The couple rang the zoo keeper, who said, 'Yes, there's space at our zoo. In fact we have a family of elephants who will welcome another one!' They arranged for Hercules to visit the zoo a few times to get used to it. Hercules felt hurt that the man and lady didn't want him any more but knew his new family of elephants understood him better, so that made him feel happier. At Zoo School, everyone was friendly at first, but after a while, other creatures stopped paying attention to Hercules. In fact, they seemed to carry on as though he wasn't there. Yet the more he trumpeted, the less they appeared to like him! Hercules grew more and more unhappy!

One day, a visitor noticed a sad looking young elephant at the edge of the enclosure. She threw a sticky bun to Hercules who sniffed it but didn't eat it at first. Hercules guessed it would be stale like so many of the leftovers that people brought. The visitor called out 'What's the matter?' She sounded kind, so Hercules decided to taste the bun after all. It was delicious! The visitor waited while he ate it, then called out again. Hercules shambled over and began telling her his troubles and misadventures. He told her his mum had wandered off, which had led him to live in a little house with strange people in a strange land. Then Hercules recalled jungle fires and horrid smelly creatures luring his mum away. Tears welled in his eyes from remembering how lonely and scared he'd been.

When Hercules finished, the visitor said, 'You are the bravest creature I ever met! What an extraordinary story! Fancy being able to survive all those adventures! You must be strong and clever as well as brave!' Hercules began to feel warm inside but said he didn't think he was at all clever. Yet the visitor insisted that he was. 'Look how well you've turned out!' she said. 'You just need to feel your own power inside you!' After that, she came back every day to talk to Hercules.

At first, Hercules found it hard to believe the nice things she said about him, but bit by bit he realised that he was a survivor and could tell some good stories. Hercules began to make more friends once he discovered that he was good at listening as well.

People say that elephants never forget! Hercules did not forget his scary times as a young elephant but he used them to tell lots of exciting stories. As he grew up, Hercules became a famous and gifted storyteller!

Discussion points

- Hercules was very brave, wasn't he? It's hard for children when they have to fend for themselves! I wonder how they cope?

- Hercules had to eat lots of nasty things just to stay alive. Did you ever feel so hungry that you ate something that tasted nasty? What was it like?

- Hercules followed the man to his house. Sometimes children are taken from their parents, but don't know why. Did anyone explain it to you?

- Hercules was embarrassed that he couldn't work out how to use the toilet. Did you find anything tricky? How did you work out what to do?

- School life was difficult for Hercules as the others didn't understand him. How do children cope if they are asked questions about their life that they don't know how to answer?

- Do you think children struggle to understand their feelings at times?

- At the zoo, Hercules felt lonely and hated being stared at. Do you think some children who are fostered or adopted feel like that too?

- Why did Hercules feel better when he told the visitor about his life? What do you think helped him most?

Activity

- With finger puppets or toy animals, play a scene in which new creatures arrive at a zoo. Explore how the others react to them.

LOW SELF-ESTEEM

Reason for referral
In foster care, Trina rejected all attempts to befriend her.

History
Trina, aged 13, believed that she was intrinsically bad. She alienated her carers in the way she herself had been alienated; in fact, she knew no other way to relate to people. Trina's birth mother had favoured Trina's younger siblings and had feigned illness to win sympathetic attention and get Trina, the eldest, to do most of the cooking and cleaning. Her mother had lived with a succession of partners who had been ill-tempered and violent towards the children. Most of the family members had learning disabilities and, like the witch whose scrambled eggs turned into vile-tasting custard, had not experienced a quality of nurture on which they could draw.

The story
This story about Wizzy the Witch illustrates how repeated abuse can affect self-esteem. Trina acknowledged that she, like Wizzy, had had to "put up or shut up". Not daring to complain, she repressed any sign of pain or frustration to avoid incurring further disapproval. Just as foster children learn new survival strategies, Wizzy and her sister witches learn new tricks at their new coven.

At their first home, the family bath had always been full of rubbish so Trina had no idea how to wash her hair until entering foster care when she was 12. Yet she insisted that the social worker was wrong to leave her in care and yearned to go home. The story ends hopefully to illustrate that recovery is possible.

Outcome
Trina began to enjoy new nurturing experiences.

Wizzy the brave witch

Once upon a time there lived a witch called Wizzy who was mostly good but believed she was bad because everything in her life had gone horribly wrong. 'It's my fault!' cried Wizzy. Her mother always said it was, although it wasn't.

When Wizzy was still a very young witch, well before she started at Witch Academy, her mother met up with some dodgy wizards. Their broomsticks clashed as every argument led to a fight. Snap! 'Oh no! That's another broomstick broken and it's your fault!' screamed Wizzy's mum at Wizzy, who cried, 'But I haven't even learned how to make spells work yet!' Her cries were drowned out by thunderclaps and torrential rain as the fights between her mum and the wizards raged on.

Then Wizzy had a new baby-witch sister, and then another! Wizzy's mum hadn't learned many good tricks at Witch Academy. Sometimes her attempts at scrambled eggs turned into the vilest tasting custard! 'Well, you'll just have to eat cold baked beans instead!' she screeched when her youngsters complained. Wizzy learned that if she needed something, she had to get it herself and usually see to the younger witches too, as they were too little to help much. 'It's hard work scrubbing broomsticks and dirty plates!' said Wizzy. Her mother snarled, 'You shouldn't have made them dirty then, should you!' as she lay on the sofa, with her feet up, pretending to be ill. Wizzy could hardly believe her ears! How can you eat without making plates dirty? But she daren't complain or she'd get a broomstick whisked around her ears! That hurt, like when her mum screamed horrid things at her over and over again.

Luckily a sorcerer heard of Wizzy's plight. The sorcerer took Wizzy and her little sister witches to a new coven. Here, the witch in charge said, 'There's the bathroom. Clean yourselves up!' Wizzy had to work out what to do. No one had ever shown her how to use a shower to wash her hair before! It was tricky, but eventually she got the hang of it. Meanwhile, Wizzy kept hoping her mother would realise how many mistakes she'd made and come to get her, but she didn't. Sometimes Wizzy cried herself to sleep wishing her mother loved her more.

One day, Wizzy moved to another coven. Here, there was so much kindness that it helped her to learn lots of good spells at home and in her new Witch Academy. Wizzy made friends with the other witches and they loved to listen to her stories about her life and how things had got better.

Discussion points

- Even though she looked after her little sisters, Wizzy believed she was bad! I wonder why? She believed her mum. Do you think children always believe what their mum tells them?

- Some nasty wizards frightened the young witches. Sometimes that happens to children in families. Who should protect the children?

- If children are scared, who can they turn to? Do you have anyone to talk to about your worries? Are there people you can trust?

- Wizzy had to do lots of cooking and cleaning. Do you think that's fair? What kind of jobs should children do? What would be unfair?

- At the coven, Wizzy didn't know how to use the shower. It can be very embarrassing not knowing how to do things. Has that ever happened to you? How did you cope?

- When Wizzy moved to the next coven, everything changed. What do you think helped? Is it useful for children to tell their story to someone?

Activity

- Make witches' hats and invent funny spells.

"SHUTTING DOWN"

Reason for referral

Mark, aged ten, acted destructively, yet rarely cried. Instead, he seemed to have "shut down". He often refused to speak to his adoptive parents, who had become worn out trying to communicate with him and frustrated by behaviour they found hard to understand. Mark struggled to share attention and needled his brothers constantly. Still loyal to his birth mother, he refused to accept that she had been unable to keep him safe.

History

Having survived parental substance misuse, domestic violence and horrific neglect, Mark was trying to protect himself from painful truths. His birth mother had been too preoccupied and stressed to pay him adequate attention.

The story

Mark loved boats. He connected with the child's experiences in *The escape from the storm*, which shows how a mother's predicaments can militate against her capacity to respond to her children. The boat tossing and turning represents the storms of life that, for Mark, had led to being hurt in violent episodes, moving house very often, and never being able to predict when he would be safe, fed or comforted. The coastguard (like a social worker) arranges for the abandoned children to live with people who will love and nurture them. In this safe and comfortable environment, they thrive.

Outcome

Enacting this story led to Mark accepting the positive ending and that his adoptive placement gave him comfort and safety. Narrating the child's fears allowed Mark to recognise and work through his own.

The escape from the storm

Once upon a time, a baby was born and named Ben. He and his mother lived in a boat built for three people, but his father dived out and swam away. At first, the sun shone and Ben's mummy thought her baby boy was wonderful. She kissed him and told him she would teach him how to swim. But a black cloud blew over and waves started rippling, then rising higher and higher. Scared they would sink, Mummy tried baling out the water. The roar of the waves was so loud that she didn't hear her baby crying. Lightning crackled across the sky as the storm erupted in full force. The baby felt cold and terribly lonely.

A pirate ship came by. The captain saw the pretty lady on board the little boat that appeared to be in trouble. Being a charmer and out for what he could get, the captain helped Mummy to climb aboard, with Ben strapped tightly to her side. The captain poured some wine, which tasted past its best, but was better than nothing since Mummy hadn't had a drink for days! They made friends and he persuaded her to stay and scrub the decks, promising "treasures" if she helped him. She worked hard day and night trying to keep the ship clean, though the pirates kept making worse and worse messes.

Then Mummy realised that the treasure she was expecting was another baby. The pirate captain was none too pleased to have two babies on board, as now, no cleaning was being done! He yelled all sorts of curses. Frightened, Mummy jumped ship, with her babies tied to her side. They swam until they found their little boat, caught on the rocks, held fast with seaweed. They sailed to another ocean through many storms, the boat rocking and rolling like Billy-O. The children felt sick but when they cried, Mummy was too busy trying to navigate the boat so they wouldn't drown. They grew invisible skins like wetsuits to protect themselves from stinging waves and their tired mummy's temper.

Eventually they reached land. Mummy stopped to rest and search for food. She made friends with crabs that stuck their claws into her. The crabs persuaded her to try special delicacies that made her feel happier for a while, but turned out to be poisonous. Just then, Daddy sailed by and snatched Ben who kept turning to look for Mummy, wishing she would come and get him.

One day, she came to collect Ben. They sailed off, glad to be together again, but the peace didn't last. A black cloud heralded another storm making the boat toss and turn. Again, the pirate ship came past. The captain grabbed the children so Mummy had to follow. She was scared but didn't know what else to do so she carried on scrubbing the decks. Then, another baby came along. With three children, Mummy couldn't stand scrubbing other people's muck any longer, so again, she strapped the babies to her and jumped ship. But this time, the pirate captain followed her, making huge waves, getting them all soaked and filthy with bilge water, and terrifying them with his vile threats and curses.

Luckily some coastguards cruised past and sent the pirate ship away. But now Mummy was so worn out, she just kept sleeping. The coastguard found a safe harbour. People in one of the moored boats agreed to look after the children until the coastguard decided what would be best.

After searching a while, he found a mummy and daddy who had always lived in strong boats and knew how to keep children safe. They sat in the warm sunshine to peel off the children's suffering skins and fill them with love and lots of amazingly yummy treats. The three boys lived with their new family in a safe harbour where they could play in their boat, protected from frightening storms and pirates of the high seas.

They went to the harbour school and took navigation lessons to learn how to sail. Ben became a skilled navigator. He didn't want to take the kind of risks his first mum had taken, so he decided that when he was grown up he would build himself a safe, sturdy boat. But sometimes, in his dreams, he found himself in the old sad boat, tossing and turning. He remembered being cold, wet and frightened in the storms. He worried about his first mum, but also felt cross that she had not looked after him better. He had bad dreams of the pirate captain coming to look for him, but was scared to talk about them in case that made it happen for real.

As time went on, Ben heard other stories of people escaping the clutches of pirates, and he began to write stories about his own experiences and escapades. Everyone admired Ben's strength and skill as he grew up. He became famous for his wisdom and understanding and was a happy man.

Discussion points

- How do you think the baby felt when his mum didn't hear him crying?

- What was life like for Ben when he lived on the pirate ship? How do you think he got on with the cruel captain? What might the other pirates have been like?

- When Ben's mum had more children, how did it affect Ben?

- The coastguard took the children to a sunny harbour. Do you think they liked it? What do you think might have worried or scared them?

- Even after Ben felt safe in his new family, he had nightmares about the past. Do you think that happens to lots of children? What would help?

Activity

- Make boats and islands using play materials, or drawing them on paper. One island could be barren, one plentiful. What do the people need to go from one to the other?

CLINGING TO THE PAST

Reason for referral

Tim, aged four, was placed for adoption but could not settle with his new family.

History

Having been in several foster placements, Tim expected to keep moving on. His last foster carer had treated him as far older than his years. Reluctant to let him go, she had sent him to his adoptive placement with a vast crate of photograph albums and memorabilia that Tim spent hours poring over. He showed no interest in the toys and games his new parents bought him. They drew a map of his journey to help Tim understand why he was living with them but he kept sending the toy cars back to "Nanny's house", even proposing that they could have Nanny's "new children" instead! Tim's belief was that he had been taken from people he trusted to this new family who seemed to want him to forget the past. He was still in shock.

The story

The story begins with Barney as a new baby bear, born to a family that finds itself in difficulty, a situation that soon becomes unsafe for Barney and the other cubs. It shows why the cubs were separated and why Barney, a brown bear, sent to live with polar bears, had to leave them too. The story addresses the pain of loss, and why it makes it difficult for children to reattach. It looks at how children can get "stuck" in the past and how they can be helped to move on.

Outcome

Tim's adoptive parents were advised to buy shelves to display Tim's new toys. On the day it was planned to tell him the story, they moved his memorabilia box into their wardrobe before he came back from school. Though it was incorporated into his life history, after hearing the story, Tim stopped asking for the box and began to explore other activities.

Barney's burden

Once upon a time, there lived a cute little bear called Barney. His mummy and daddy adored him. 'Barney will be a good friend for his big brother,' they said. At first, everything went well. The bears went for walks showing Barney off to their friends. Winter came. The weather turned colder and it was harder to keep their cave warm. Daddy Bear went off hunting while Mummy Bear tried to keep her cubs fed and cosy. Mummy Bear thought Daddy Bear had the best job, as he was meeting other animals and having fun. But Daddy Bear thought Mummy Bear had the best job, because she was at home! They argued and fought. Being big and heavy, they hurt each other, forgetting that their little cubs were watching and felt scared. Sometimes the cubs got bruised as well.

One day, Barney found Mummy Bear lying slumped in a corner of the cave. Barney was afraid she would never wake up. Too little to know what to do, he cried his heart out. Hearing his cries, a kind deer sent a message to Barney's relatives to see who could help, but there was only Granny Bear and she was too poorly. The deer asked who else could help. A family of beavers said they looked after young animals when parents were not able to.

And so Barney and his brother went to the Beaver family. Barney's brother blamed Barney for their having to leave home and kept punching him. Deciding that it would be safer for them to live in different families, Deer took Barney to a family of polar bears. Nanny Polar Bear gave him lots of treats and made him feel very important. But he was given too many grown-up jobs to do, like opening the door to visitors, when all Barney wanted was to be little and looked after, and play. The deer knew that the polar bears couldn't keep Barney because polar bears live in cold places. Barney needed somewhere warmer! Finally, she found a family of antelopes with coats close in colour to Barney's brown fur. Their huge antlers would protect him from harm. The antelopes had a cosy home and the deer knew they would love Barney and care for him until he was grown up.

But Barney had many treasures that he couldn't bear to leave behind. He packed them on a sleigh, which became too heavy to pull. On the way, he met Olly Owl who was amazed at how tired Barney looked. 'Let me help you pull that sleigh,' said Olly. Barney thanked him. Olly wrapped his talons around the reins but the sleigh was too heavy, so he flew off to get more help. Fred Fox tried to help but hardly budged it. Fred asked Willy Weasel to lend a hand, only to hear him say, 'Why not take some of the treasures off? We'll put them in a safe place. You'll get to your new home quicker if you have less to carry.' Barney was getting tired, so he took off the heaviest treasures and was thrilled at how light the sleigh was!

On reaching his new home, Barney discovered that he liked the antelope family. Though he missed Nanny Polar Bear and hoped she missed him too, Barney knew he was lucky because his new mummy and daddy adored him and wanted to keep him safe and happy.

Discussion points

- When Mummy and Daddy Bear argued, the cubs were scared. The deer knew the bear cubs needed to be safe. How do you think Barney and his brother felt when they were taken to live with a new family?

- Do brothers often fight? How should grown-ups protect littler ones?

- Barney was very young when Nanny Polar Bear sent him to open the door to visitors. At what age should children answer the door or phone?

- The antelopes' fur was the same colour as Barney's. Is it important for children to look like their parents? Does it help? If so, how?

- Barney held on to his treasures. Why were they so important?

- How did he feel when he took the heaviest ones off the sleigh?

Activity

- Use clay or play dough to make bears and a sleigh; draw the homes they live in.

TRAUMA

Reason for referral

Darren and Jaydon, aged seven and four years, were traumatised not only by the neglect they experienced but also by their mother's attempts to abduct them from care.

History

The boys had suffered abuse while at home and had been placed in care. Their mother then abducted them from care and attempted to set fire to the foster home. Back in care, the children banged their heads and rocked themselves as a form of self-comfort. Like "rabbits caught in headlights", they were easily startled and their trauma had led them to have poor bowel control.

The story

The young rabbits suffer adversity that parallels the boys' experience. In winter, food shortages leave them hungry. Their parent rabbits meet creatures who encourage the excessive drinking of cowslip wine (symbolising alcohol abuse). These parent rabbits squabble bitterly, part and find new partners, leaving Mickey and Jay to survive as best they can. The kindness of the squirrel who rescues them conveys that adults *can* be trustworthy. The wise owl, like a judge, decides that because Mummy Rabbit cannot use advice, her bunnies need safe creatures to look after them. While in the Badgers' family where, like children taken to new homes, they have to get used to new rules and new food, Mummy Rabbit tried to steal them but eventually they are found a place where they can be safe.

Outcome

The story helped Darren and Jaydon to realise that their parents had failed to protect them when they had been too young to protect themselves. They could identify with the plight of the bunnies feeling cold, dirty and hungry and their burrow smelly with droppings. Eventually, they made a successful transition to their permanent placement.

A safe place for Mickey and Jay

Once upon a time, there lived a family of rabbits in a peaceful woodland copse. Mummy Rabbit's baby, Mickey, had the softest fur and the loveliest eyes you could ever imagine. Mummy Rabbit was thrilled with her baby who nuzzled up close to her. She licked him all over, to keep him clean.

Winter came and it was cold. The wet leaves on the ground covered the nuts and berries, so the rabbits were hungry. Cold and fed up, Mummy Rabbit went off in search of comfort. Weasels let her stay in their warm burrow, but Daddy Rabbit was cross with Mummy Rabbit for not looking after baby Mickey. She moaned, 'You're always horrid to me! Leave me alone!' Mummy Rabbit went off to find friends who were nice to her. The weasels gave her lots of cowslip wine, which made her sleepy. It made her forget that she had a baby to look after!

As he grew, Mickey learned to hunt for food. One day, a big crow flew off with him. Frightened and hurt, poor Mickey was dropped into a muddy stream. Well, everyone knows that rabbits don't like water! His fur became matted and dirty. Then he ate the wrong kind of berries, which made him sick. A snake rubbed against Mickey who froze, terrified. Luckily, a squirrel scrambled down from her tree and surprised the snake, which slithered off into the undergrowth.

Mummy Rabbit made friends with a new Daddy Rabbit and they all moved into another warren. Soon Mickey had a baby brother, Jay. The burrow became stuffy and smelly from droppings. Mummy Rabbit often went out for a long time, leaving Mickey to look after his baby brother. The bunnies were cold, dirty and hungry, their skin bitten and sore. A friendly squirrel saw them looking sad and thin. She told Wise Owl, who called a meeting to decide what to do. Mummy Rabbit was persuaded to go to Beech Wood Family Centre to learn how to look after her bunnies but she did not listen to any advice and her bunnies still had to fend for themselves. Wise Owl said the bunnies needed safe creatures to look after them, and sent them to a family of badgers.

The badgers' sett was warm and clean, with plenty of food, but it smelled different. They ate at strange times and had rules that Mickey and Jay didn't understand, like sitting down together for meals. To make life even more complicated, Mummy Rabbit kept trying to steal the bunnies back. They never knew whether they were coming or going!

Squirrel decided the bunnies needed to be where Mummy Rabbit couldn't find them, so took them to a family of voles in a distant wood. Here, mice and rats weaved in and out all day long. Jay kept crying and Mickey still worried about Mummy Rabbit finding them. The voles were too busy to pay them much attention.

Squirrel carried on searching until she found a family of rabbits who would take good care of them. She took Mickey and Jay to their new home where they were well fed and had fun playing. They grew beautiful glossy coats, and stopped worrying.

· ·

Discussion points

- Mummy Rabbit loved her babies but the fights scared her bunnies. Why do you think they fought?
- Mickey was frightened of the crow and snake. Why do you think he was scared? What things do you find scary?
- Like Mickey, some children have to find their own food. What is it like to be hungry and have nothing to eat? What might you eat?
- How do children learn to keep themselves clean, e.g. brushing their teeth and washing?
- Did Wise Owl make the right decision? What would you have done?
- Do you think Mummy Rabbit was given enough help/chances?
- How can parents help children feel safe and welcome?

Activity

- Using string, twigs and leaves, make a little woodland shelter.

Stories introduce children to the topic of why they are in care in a gentle way that enables them to process horrific experiences while feeling supported in a safe family. In relating to the experiences of fictional heroes, children are able to make connections to their own stories and cease blaming themselves for their rejection and abandonment. New parents, who reach a deeper understanding of how their children experienced their earlier life, are enabled to support their children more effectively.

Stories to address specific problems

3

The stories in this chapter address a variety of problems faced by children who have difficulty trusting their new parents or sustaining friendships. The stories are brief, because the children are often too anxious to concentrate. The aim is to gently introduce the language of "feelings" to children whose way of relating can present as superficial and precarious. But as many will have learned to sublimate their needs, these stories avoid a sentimental emphasis on emotions to which children do not or cannot relate and may dismiss as "weird" or "embarrassing". Children will connect with the stories because they are about "someone else" and absorb messages that have resonance for them.

How to use the stories

Stories can be enjoyed for their implicit messages without adults having to spell out their literal meaning to the child. Recurrent patterns in children's play reveal their preoccupations with themes such as "good versus bad" or "trust versus betrayal". Metaphors connect physical and emotional states. Hence, we may speak of being "choked with emotion" or of "jumping for joy". Effectively, metaphor acts as a "bridge" between the logical left and emotional right hemispheres of the brain, and language helps to bring feelings to our consciousness and guides us in how to manage them (Damasio, 1998).

Each of the stories below is preceded by a case example to explain the connections it had for the child. Parents and carers are encouraged to read the story and, provided that the child reacts with interest, use the discussion points that follow to talk about its content, preferably through involving the child in a creative activity. Children may be embarrassed to admit to their strong feelings, yet will generally respond to an activity-based approach (using sensory materials and experimenting with materials, textures and sounds) that does not depend on verbal language but brings their pre-verbal experience to consciousness so that long-standing fears can be mitigated. When parents praise and admire their activities and ideas, children who might otherwise give up quickly are motivated to persist and this helps them develop skills in problem solving.

. . . .

THEME: FEELING WORTHLESS, ANGRY

Source of problem
The first story was written for a child aged nine, in long-term foster care, whose early experience of violence led him to believe that he was intrinsically "bad". His rejection by his birth mother was followed by multiple moves in care.

The metaphor
The child's belief is personified by the pumpkin who thinks he is evil because of the way he is treated. When "lit", the pumpkin displays a grimace, as might anyone who is feeling angry, but it frightens the children. It can be difficult to hide our feelings and easy to forget that anger and rage can often mask a sense of powerlessness. Like the neglected child, the pumpkin feels "empty and hollow". Adults sometimes complain of their child giving them "evil" looks and attribute illogically a degree of power to the child, failing to recognise how scared the child may feel but be unable to articulate. If we view people negatively, they respond as we expect. Feeling discarded, the pumpkin too desires revenge for maltreatment and abandonment. But a creative gesture turns things around! A child plants the discarded seeds, which grow into new pumpkins to be enjoyed in play. The story concludes with the pumpkin becoming convinced of its self-worth after all. A key message to give to the child is that he is loveable even though his birth parents had not been very good at loving him or keeping him safe.

The pumpkin who thought he was evil

Once upon a time, there was a large pumpkin growing on a farm. When it was nearly Hallowe'en, the farmer sold it to a family nearby. The children tried to cut out a face, but as the pumpkin had grown very large, they found it hard to cut into, so their parents helped. The pumpkin had lots of seeds, which they scooped out until it was empty and hollow. For the pumpkin, losing all his stuffing wasn't a nice feeling at all! Dad cut out wide scary eyes, a big triangular nose and a very angry looking mouth. He placed a lit candle inside the pumpkin. But the children, seeing the lit up pumpkin pulling a horrible face at them, shrieked with fear. The pumpkin, fearing that he really must be scary, began to think he was evil.

That night, the family had a party. They put a hat on the pumpkin, placed it on the windowsill and left the candle burning inside it all night long. Lots of people screamed at the sight of the pumpkin but that was part of the fun of Hallowe'en! The pumpkin became charred inside, which made him even more certain that he was rotten!

The next day, Dad threw the pumpkin out onto a heap of smelly compost. For the pumpkin, this was proof that he was evil. The pumpkin started to go mouldy and smelly. 'Phew! What a stink!' said Mother, wrinkling her nose: 'That pumpkin's no use even to make soup!' The pumpkin was angry: 'They hate me! My life has been wasted!' He wanted revenge!

Just then, one of the children caught sight of the pumpkin and asked what had happened to the pumpkin seeds. 'They're in the bin!' replied Mother. The child scooped the seeds out of the bin and planted them to see if any would grow. He then moved the pumpkin to the patio, filled it with soil and planted a hyacinth bulb inside. Next spring the bulb flowered. As the hyacinth smelled so lovely, the mother brought the pumpkin back into the house. Now the old pumpkin felt pleased because he was welcome once again and he smelled lovely. He was even more pleased to see new little pumpkins growing from his seeds. It made him think that he wasn't that bad after all!

Discussion points

- The pumpkin felt empty when its seeds were removed. What makes children feel empty?

- When children feel sad, how can we make them feel better?

- The large pumpkin was especially hard to cut into. The children needed their parents' help. What kind of things do you need help with?

- The pumpkin was angry at being charred on the inside. What makes children angry? Does it help to be listened to?

- The pumpkin's expression frightened the children. Was the pumpkin being angry or was it something else? Have you seen a frightened look on someone's face? What made them scared? Were you able to reassure them?

- The pumpkin hated being thrown out. Children who can't live with their parents can feel rejected and angry. What might help them?

- When he got taken back into the house the old pumpkin was very pleased. What do you think helps children to feel that they belong? How can their family and friends help them feel wanted?

Activities

- Cut out facial features into two hollowed out pumpkins and have the two pumpkins have a "dialogue" about how they feel as a "pumpkin".

- Paint pumpkin seeds and thread them to make a necklace or collage.

- Encourage the child to make a card for someone special, using the pumpkin seeds to create the shape of a heart or star.

THEME: FEELING OUT OF CONTROL

Source of problem

This story was designed to help a distressed child to recognise and understand the source of his out-of-control behaviour. As an infant, Kyle had been left strapped in a chair or playpen for hours, so had not developed the agility of others of his age who could climb and explore. On the receiving end of his parents' persistent criticism, for reasons he did not understand, Kyle, like Teddy the tank engine, found it difficult to "stay on track".

The metaphor

The story shows that when the little train did not receive the quality of care it needed to be able to work properly, its engine became stiff with rust. This left the train unable to move, which, in turn, upset the passengers. The driver got frustrated and reacted by over-oiling Teddy's wheels so that the little train couldn't stop and crashed.

In this respect, Teddy is like a child who needs nurture in order to function properly. Children can rapidly project their insecurity on to the adults around them, and make everyone feel as powerless as they do. When threatened, we seek someone to blame. For example, at the railway yard, the stationmaster remonstrated with the driver who would not accept responsibility for the accident and blamed his accuser. Yet when Teddy was taken to a place where mechanics (like substitute carers) had proper training, his engine was looked after properly and restored to capacity.

This story will encourage children in care to realise that, with improved nurture, they too will develop their potential to meet or even exceed expectations.

The train that couldn't stay on track

Once upon a time, there was a tank engine called Teddy because the cute face of a teddy was painted on his front. Teddy the Tank Engine was sturdy, but the station guards didn't always remember to oil his joints and when they did, they often poured on far too much, which made Teddy's wheels skid. It meant that Teddy was often slow to start or found it hard to stop on time. This would make the driver get cross and shout at Teddy, even though it was never Teddy's fault at all.

One day, no one had remembered to oil Teddy's joints, which made him late getting started. It took the driver such a long time to rev up the engine that the passengers began to shout and complain! Upset, the driver revved the engine as hard as he could but Teddy was too stiff to move! The driver got out to fetch oil and poured it all over Teddy's joints. Everyone, except Teddy, heaved a sigh of relief as the train took off. As I expect you can guess, the driver had poured on far too much oil so Teddy struggled to keep his slippery wheels on the track.

Soon they were approaching a barrier. A red signal warned the driver to stop. The train driver tried to brake but Teddy didn't stop! Teddy couldn't stop! His wheels were far too oily so he just kept going and crashed through the barrier at breakneck speed! Bits of gate flew everywhere. Luckily, no one was hurt. The driver realised that Teddy's wheels were now too oily, so he stopped the train as they went up a hill. The passengers had to wait while the driver cleaned Teddy's wheels.

Back at the railway yard, the stationmaster was cross. He yelled, 'You could have caused a terrible accident!' The driver shouted back, 'It's not my fault! If you looked after the train properly, this would never have happened!'

Teddy the Tank Engine was taken to a train shed where the mechanics had been trained to look after train engines properly. Teddy's wheels and joints were properly cleaned and oiled. Soon his body was being polished until it was gleaming and his engine put in good working order. Now Teddy performed so well that the railway company put him on display as their best engine and people queued to have a special ride! The driver loved telling stories about Teddy's adventures.

Discussion points

● Teddy got his name because his front looked like a teddy! Do you know how you got your name and what your name means?

● Teddy the Tank Engine was sturdily built but the people at the railway yard did not take good care of him. What care did Teddy need? How did Teddy feel when his engine ran out of oil?

- Teddy hated it when the passengers shouted crossly. We all hate being shouted at. Do you think Teddy is like a real person in this way?

- When Teddy became rusted, it was hard for the driver to get him started. What makes life harder for you?

- When too much oil was poured on Teddy's wheels, he couldn't stop. How do you think Teddy felt when his wheels kept skidding?

- At times we all feel cross and might say or do things we don't mean. What is the best thing to do when that happens?

- When Teddy was well looked after, he was put on display and gave rides. What helps children to do well? What help would you like?

Activity

- You can enact an activity using a train set. But if you don't have one, you can draw Teddy the Tank Engine onto card and cut it out. On long pieces of plain wallpaper, draw a train track and station. Make traffic lights and barriers from card and colour them. With toy people, enact the next chapter of Teddy's adventures. The child can invent more characters, with encouragement from his or her parent.

THEME: FEELING INVISIBLE

Source of problem

When parents are depressed and emotionally inaccessible, their children may instinctively repress their own feelings as the only safe means of survival. A young girl called Daisy believed that her needs didn't matter so long as she took care of her depressed mother's feelings. Now in care, Daisy felt "invisible". She had not learned to notice changes in temperature or to distinguish between tastes, textures or smells. The following story helped her match physical sensations to her emotions.

The metaphor

In the story, the child learns that, because doors are stiff, she will gain more comfort from sitting on a soft chair than leaning against a hard surface. The sofa advises her that 'the more you sink in, the softer and comfier you will be'.

Like many neglected children, the heroine's response to questions is 'I don't know!' This is a safe and accurate answer that relieves children of making choices for which they feel ill-equipped but one that can infuriate adults trying to accommodate their wishes. In common with many young children in care, the child has not learned to tell the time, so the clock shows her when it's teatime. On noticing the inviting smells, the child realises that she feels hungry.

Children who are used to frightening or unwelcome sensations may not be very familiar with pleasurable, healthy stimulation. In this story, the kindly foster mother acts in a gentle, nurturing manner to help the girl feel wanted and admired for having learned to notice feelings that she can welcome rather than fear. To give such children hope for their future, the story conveys that life for this child will continue to improve.

The child who learned she had feelings

Once upon a time, there was a girl called Crystal who had no feelings. At least she didn't think she had any. Having had a rough time, she'd learned to bury them deep down inside her. One day, Crystal came to live in a new family. As she stood leaning against the door, it spoke to her. 'I'm very stiff, as you might notice. You may prefer to sit down rather than lean against me for too long!' Surprised, the child asked, 'Why are you stiff?' The door replied, 'I just get bored listening to people all day long!'

Puzzled, Crystal went into the sitting room and bounced onto a big squashy sofa. The sofa made a squeaky sound as it groaned gently. 'Phew! I wasn't expecting that! Anyway, welcome to the comfy zone! Are you sitting comfortably?' Crystal said, 'I don't know!' That was her reply to most things she was asked! 'Well, I'll explain!' said the sofa. 'The more you sink into me, the softer and comfier you will be! Now, are you feeling soft and comfy?' 'Yes!' said Crystal, 'Good!' said the sofa.

As she snuggled down, she heard a clock ticking. She looked at the numbers on the clock but didn't know what they meant, as no one had ever taught her to tell the time. Crystal wondered when she would get something to eat. As if hearing her thoughts, the clock chimed: 'It's nearly teatime. When both my arms hit the number at the bottom, you'll know it's time to eat!' She looked again. She saw one clock arm on the six and the other arm close by. Just then, the second arm clicked on to the six and the clock chimed a tune. 'Teatime!' called Mother from the kitchen.

Crystal noticed a warm appetising smell wafting into the room. 'Hungry?' asked Mother. Crystal nodded. 'We are having spaghetti bolognaise followed by chocolate cake. Would you like that?' asked Mother. 'Yes!' replied Crystal, shyly. Mother said, 'I hope you will be happy in this house! They told me you haven't had many nice times but we'll try to make up for that! Feelings are very important in this house!' Crystal told her, 'I know the door feels stiff, the sofa feels soft, and your clock told me when it's time to eat!' Admiringly, the mother said, 'That's amazing! You've only been here a few minutes and already you've learned such a lot!'

Strangely, the furniture stopped talking after that, but now Crystal knew there were some feelings inside her that she no longer needed to be frightened of. Some were especially nice, like when Mother gave her hugs and hot chocolate!

Discussion points

- The child in the story didn't think she had any feelings. Which parts of your body tell you what you are feeling? Can you name the feelings?

- Crystal learnt that the door felt stiff and the sofa felt soft. Where is your favourite place to sit, where you feel most comfortable?

- Crystal didn't know how to tell the time. I wonder how that made her feel. It must make life confusing! How do children learn to tell the time?

- At first, Crystal didn't know she was hungry. What made her realise? What is your favourite food? What smells do you like best?

- Crystal used to be scared of feelings. Do you think that is why she didn't want to notice them? What do you think would help her?

- Are there feelings that you don't like or are scared of? What would help you not be scared of them any longer?

Activity

- Make facial features out of newspaper such as eyes, nose, mouth and ears. Tack/stick them to the door, cupboards and furniture. Give each face a name such as Charlie Chair, Dora Door, Sally Sofa. Have a conversation with them. See if it develops into a story. Each character might have a problem that the others can help with.

THEME: SEXUAL ABUSE

Source of problem

Many children who are taken into public care have been sexually abused. They may not know they were being abused, or know what is "normal" until they are able to compare their experience with that of others. Young children who have become sexualised can become physically dependent on stimulation and crave to be close to people, confusing their attachment needs with physical urges. They need supervision and activities that provide healthier stimulation (Corrigan and Moore, 2011). Some children experience isolated instances of sexual abuse whereas others are subjected to them frequently and can be involved in a variety of sexual activities. Frequent moves can make children accustomed to being "nice" to everyone, in the hope that someone will reciprocate. They may be excessively friendly and some are indiscriminate in their craving for attention.

The metaphor

The story of the pretty flower can help abused children recognise the need for self-protection. Fleur's strong stem represents her inner strength and instinct for survival. When the mother flower is destroyed, Fleur forgets to close her petals at night and is invaded by creepy crawlies that leave her battered and droopy with the effort of coping with their weight. Traumatised children often dread night time when it reminds them of former abuse. Fleur is transplanted to another corner of the garden where the soil is better (conveying that a move to improved care gives children greater protection and nurture). The more mature flowers express their concern for Fleur and teach her how to protect herself. The gardener, like a parent, expresses pride in Fleur's beauty and success.

The pretty flower

Once upon a time, behind a rambling old house there was an untidy garden full of weeds and wild flowers. Among them, a very pretty flower sprang up, named Fleur by her mother flower. Fleur had an especially strong stem, which is why this delicate flower survived in the wild garden. A more fragile flower would probably have been strangled by weeds and died an early death. When the sun came out, the pretty flower spread her petals in the way her mother had taught her, to catch the raindrops when she was thirsty and to let the sun warm her.

One day, the rambling old house was sold. A gardener dug up many of the flowers tangled in amongst the weeds, including Fleur's parent flowers. Now Fleur was lonely. She missed her parents and had no one to lean on or share her thoughts with. Being a brave, sturdy flower, Fleur kept her petals open. As the weather turned cold and wet, beetles and slugs crawled into the open flower at night. These insects were slimy, and some smelt very unpleasant indeed! The little flower became tired and tattered with the effort of holding these heavy and unwelcome creatures. Fleur began to dread nightfall. Her petals drooped.

One sunny day, two children were playing in the garden when they saw Fleur. 'Oh! Isn't she pretty!' said the girl. 'But her petals are torn!' said the boy. 'Perhaps this soil doesn't suit her! Let's take her to our allotment!'

Carefully they dug up the little flower and carried her tenderly to another part of the garden where the soil was lighter, for growing herbs and vegetables. 'Here you are, little flower!' said the boy, planting her in a sunny spot. They took a photo of Fleur, who felt rather proud. 'But she's all by herself!' said the girl. She and her brother found some healthy flowers and planted them next to Fleur. 'There, now you have company!' said the children, particularly pleased with their efforts.

Fleur was happy in her new surroundings. But as the seasons went by, the bigger flowers noticed that she kept her petals open all the time. There were fewer slugs here, but worms and beetles still slithered around. The bigger flowers gave her some good advice: 'When the sun goes down you need to close your petals like this. They will protect you in the dark and in cold weather. Watch how we do it!' And so at last Fleur learned to furl her petals at night, like the other flowers.

Fleur grew stronger and more beautiful as the days went by. The gardener took pictures of her and won prizes. Soon Fleur appeared in competitions, winning praise for her beauty. She led a happy life, enjoying all the attention and admiration, while keeping herself safe.

Discussion points

- Fleur lost her parent flowers when the gardener tore them up. She soon drooped. What is it like for children to lose their parents?

- Fleur kept her petals open. As a result, lots of insects crawled in. What do you think she disliked most about these insects?

- What happened to Fleur when she was moved to another part of the garden? Was she lonely?

- Do you think she wanted to move? Who helped Fleur and how?

- Why did the other flowers worry about Fleur? How did they help?

- It is really the grown-ups' job to protect children, but what can children do to protect themselves?

Activities

- Make a miniature garden in a seed tray. Tell a story about the flowers.

- Cut pictures of flowers from gardening magazines to create a collage of an ideal garden.

- Perhaps the child could plant some flowers in the garden or in a window box or plant pot and look after them.

THEME: LOSS

Source of problem

The next story was written for Simon, who was facing his first Christmas in foster care. He was miserable at having been rejected by his mother while his siblings remained at home. Like Enry Elf, Simon had intervened to protect his mother from his father's violence and had often been blamed by her for her troubles but he did not understand why. The loss of an attachment figure can cause intolerable pain, even more so when the child is having to adjust to changes in his environment. Loss and change impact on the brain's memory systems and can leave the child distressed and confused. Being no longer able to rely on his procedural memory (or "auto pilot"), normally depended on to get by, can cause feelings of shame and embarrassment likely to enhance the child's psychological pain.

The metaphor

The story describes the confusion that Enry feels when he has to move: 'The smells, food, routine, in fact, everything, felt strange'. The elf becomes confused about the order of his jobs and is flooded with shame when he makes a mistake, a predicament that is typical for children who have had inadequate reassurance (Corrigan and Moore, 2011) and low self-esteem.

Enry feels humiliated that he is unable to keep up with the other elves but brightens up when the sympathetic Santa arranges a party for all of them. (Children can similarly be reassured by contact with siblings who are placed separately.) Modelling empathy, Mother Pixie talks to Enry about his feelings, asking him what he misses most. She makes lists of events and tasks and writes them out in order to help him remember. Her understanding helps Enry to accept that he is safer in her care and to reconcile himself to his new situation.

The elf who hated Christmas

Once upon a time in the woods, there lived many families of elves and pixies. Mostly they led good lives, helping one another, but there are always some folk who find life harder than others. One such family kept arguing. Father Elf had discovered foxglove wine but when he drank too much, he turned nasty and when Mother Elf drank too much, it made her sleepy. Then Father Elf would be cross because she hadn't got his dinner ready and he would be left feeding the children. Sometimes he lost his temper and hurt his little elves, so they often hid from him.

Enry, the biggest elf, tried to look after Mum but she blamed him for all her troubles. Hearing about it, Santa tutted, 'It's wrong for parents to hurt children. And so near Christmas too – as if I didn't have enough to be doing already!' But of course Santa was a kind sort. He quickly asked around the forest for a safe home and organised his reindeers to take the little elves to some kind pixies that he knew.

Enry was separated from his brothers and sisters as there wasn't enough room in any of the toadstool homes to fit all the little elves under one roof. 'There, there, Enry, you can sleep over here!' said Mother Pixie gently, showing the tearful elf his new bed. She tried to make him welcome, but the smells, food, routine, in fact, everything…felt strange. Enry was scared of forgetting things or losing his way. He had to keep asking and it was really quite exhausting. Everyone got fed up with his questions as they expected him to know things or learn them quickly. It was too much for Enry. 'Am I supposed to pick the cowslips for soup or collect firewood first?' he wondered anxiously.

Mother Pixie was busy getting things ready for Christmas and had a lot to do. She asked Enry to find her acorns for the Christmas pudding. Enry was keen to please her but by the time he got outside he'd forgotten what she wanted and returned with a heap of brambles! 'Oh dear, now I'm going to run behind!' said Mother Pixie, a bit crossly, '…but never mind!' But Enry did mind. He felt so embarrassed, his face went red. Feeling hot and even more worried, he cried, 'I can never get anything right!'

Luckily one of Santa's helpers overheard him and told Santa, who arranged a party for Enry to see his brothers and sisters. Santa asked each elf which game they wanted and what they liked to eat. The mother pixies brought everyone's favourite food. They played everyone's favourite games, and a marvellous time was had by all! Later, Mother Pixie spoke to Enry and said, 'I want you to enjoy Christmas with us!' She asked what he missed most. Enry admitted that he missed his mum, but he also told her about how his life had been. Mother Pixie nodded. 'That's so sad! I wish I could help!'

In fact, sharing his worries made Enry feel better. Mother Pixie made a wall chart with a list of events over Christmas so Enry would know what to expect and when. She listed his jobs in order so he could check if he forgot. He stopped panicking, got on with his jobs and looked forward to eating pumpkin pie and playing games. Enry slept well over Christmas, glad he no longer had to worry about fights and having to choose between hiding his brothers and sisters or protecting his mum. But he still missed her and thought about her.

• •

Discussion points

● When Father Elf drank too much foxglove wine, he was unkind to the little elves. How did Enry try to help? What happened when he did?

● Why do you think Enry's mum blamed him? It's horrid being blamed unfairly! How can children cope if that happens?

● When Enry went to live with the pixies, he felt very confused. What did he find hardest? Have you found any changes difficult?

● Enry hated making mistakes and not being able to keep up. How can adults make things easier for children? Do lists help?

● How did the party with his brothers and sisters help?

● Enry felt better after explaining that he was missing his mum. Is there someone special that you miss or would like to talk about?

● How can adults help children sort out their muddled feelings?

Activity

● Plan games and food for a family party. Design the invitations.

• •

THEME: FEELING FRUSTRATED, INADEQUATE

Source of problem
Charmaine, aged 13, was achieving academically at around the level of a six-year-old. For many years, she and her sisters were sexually abused by their father. In her permanent placement, she wanted to change her name so as to "wash away" the "old Charmaine" and move forward with a new identity. Charmaine was receptive to learning about her history and enjoyed dramatising it, but struggled to cope with her feelings of betrayal and confusion. Consumed with rage about her abuse, she screamed for hours, scaring her younger sisters.

The metaphor
The story sets out to validate the child's entitlement to her strong feelings, firstly, by helping her to realise that they stemmed from appallingly upsetting memories; secondly, by enabling her to understand the consequences of her actions. Thus the feelings of the girl who thought she was the wind spin so far out of control that the mother's china plate breaks and her sisters become frightened. When the "storm" ends, the mother demonstrates empathy for Wind's terror, prompting her apology for scaring her little sisters. Advised on how to manage her feelings, Wind tempers her force and finds gentle breezes are more effective than tornadoes.

Charmaine was helped to find words to explain her feelings. From a selection of scarves, she chose colours to match her moods and wafted them to create "gentle breezes". Walking around the house and garden to identify the smells and sounds, tastes and textures that she enjoyed, helped her to experience a sense of belonging in her long-term foster family.

The girl who thought she was the wind

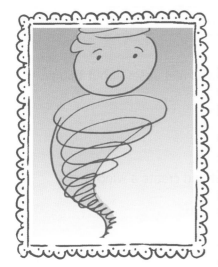

Once upon a time there was a girl who went to live with a new family. The girl danced around as she joined in the family activities: 'She's just like a breath of fresh air!' said her new parents. Hearing this, the girl thought to herself, 'I'm like the wind!' And she began to call herself Windy, though actually her real name was Wendy.

One day, Windy woke from a dream, feeling weird. She had a bad feeling in her tummy. The bad feeling got worse through the day. Everything went wrong! Soon she was feeling pretty mad. Windy started remembering things she didn't like to remember, things that made her feel very cross and upset!

As the bad feeling got stronger and stronger, the day got stormier and stormier!

Windy rushed about kicking and bashing and slamming doors until the whole house shook as if they were in the middle of a hurricane! Wham! Crash! Bang! Smash! Then came the sound of splintering as broken china hit the floor! 'That was my favourite china plate!' said Mum, sadly. But Windy replied crossly, 'It was your fault! You made me break it!' She knew that wasn't true but she was so mad, she wanted to blame someone for her bad feelings! And she wanted revenge! And she was scared!

As she saw the look on Mum's face, clouds gathered and Windy started crying. So now it was raining as well as stormy! Windy felt worse than ever!

Suddenly a rage filled her up from her tummy right up to her head. She screamed and made a very loud noise, just like a tornado! The other children hid under their beds, terrified! Mum sat on the floor waiting for the furniture to stop shaking. The tornado lasted for several hours! Suddenly it stopped – it had fizzled out. Windy lay down and slept.

The next day, the other children looked anxiously at Windy. 'Last night was scary!' they said. Mum said, 'You must be very tired!' She gave Windy a big hug. 'Sorry!' said Windy. 'I didn't mean to scare you all!' Mum helped Windy to practise breathing gently and showed her how to pick up the scents from flowers so that she wouldn't need to blow a fierce tornado again.

From then on, Windy was gentle as a breeze – well, most of the time, anyway!

• •

Discussion points

- Sometimes we misunderstand what people say. Have you ever misheard a word and thought the person meant something else?

- Wendy changed her name to Windy. Why do you think she wanted to? Do you like your name? Would you change it? If so, why and what to?

- When Windy was upset, horrid memories made her tummy hurt. Where in your body do you notice if something feels wrong?

- Windy's anger caused damage. How could she have safely shown her cross feelings? What do you do if you are feeling mad?

- The other children were scared by Windy's anger. What helped her?

- Do you think it is important that Windy said "sorry"? Why?

- Can you think of any other ways that parents can help children who feel upset about things that happened to them in the past?

Activities

- Use silk scarves or other flowing material, muslin or saris to float and create a wind that becomes a "tornado". How does the wind die down?

- Compare textures and properties of various fabrics.

- Make your own weather story, using fabrics. Paint a picture of the scenery.

- Walk around the garden or a park noticing how many different smells there are.

THEME: CONFLICT

Source of problem

Colin gets the hump was written for 10-year-old Neil, who found it difficult to back down from disputes. He would kick and punch, terrified of obliteration if he did not "win". His birth mother had been abused throughout her childhood. She had exposed him to violence and abuse and had repeatedly abandoned him. When Neil was five he was taken into care, yet he remained faithful to her. He had no internalised model for coping with challenges except through conflict. Like Colin the camel, Neil had grown his own "hump", which became harder to shift as he kept being rejected. In his latest long-term foster placement, Neil had begun to settle but he still kept falling out with his best friend, insisting that everything that went wrong was the other boy's fault.

The metaphor

The purpose of the story was firstly to explain how the camel developed his hump so that Neil could stop blaming himself for the events over which he had no control, and which had led to his removal to care. Secondly, the intention was to illustrate a strategy for managing conflict, which Neil, who was terrified of not being "perfect" (as it threatened further abandonment), could emulate, and which would enable him to back down from confrontations. To help the young camel, Colin, to retrieve and rebuild friendships, mothers of bickering camels arrange to demonstrate problem-resolution in scenarios for the young adversaries to watch together. By the end of the story, Neil realised that he wanted to make up with his friend and he sent a message of apology with his foster carer to the boy's mother.

Colin gets the hump

Once upon a time there was a camel called Colin who lived in a desert. Colin's mum had a very big hump indeed, which had grown larger because she was treated badly as a young camel. Colin loved his mother camel, but he didn't want to grow up to have as big a hump as she had grown, as it meant carrying a lot more weight, which really hurt!

In fact, his mother had become far too worn down by the weight to look after her young camel. So Colin was led to another family of camels. All was well unless any of them crossed his path…if they did, there'd be trouble! Colin had a fine pair of legs and as he kicked out, other camels with more spindly legs went flying. The parent camels soon became fed up and sent Colin away. So he kept being sent from one camel family to another.

Eventually, Colin landed up in a camel family that had only a mum and dad. Mostly, this mum and dad were kind and patient with Colin, so when he met other young camels, he frolicked happily with them and made some very good friends. The only snag was that every now and then, one of the young camels would kick Colin while they were playing. Sometimes they did it on purpose, other times by accident. But Colin could never tell if they meant to hurt him or not. So he would kick back and the fights would then begin. And go on and on! After a while Colin would stomp off, feeling his hump growing bigger and heavier by the minute. It made him feel a bit sick. Getting the hump wasn't a nice feeling at all!

One day, the mother camels met at a watering hole. 'Harrumph!' they said, chewing things over, 'If only they would say "Sorry" to each other! Then each of them could say "Didn't mean to hurt you, I still want to be friends." Then they could forget about it and have some fun!' They all agreed.

The mother camels hatched a plot. They took Colin and the camel he'd been fighting with to some rocks where they could sit while they watched a play. In the play, two camels bump into each other. One says, 'That hurt!' The other says, 'Sorry!' Then they both go off. Two more camels come on and start bickering about nothing and everything. The camels stomp off but they come back and talk over what they disagreed about and they sort it out.

After a while, Colin saw what he could do to make up with his friend. And because his friend was watching too, both wanted to make things better. So they playfully whacked their feet and tails together, tried to bump their humps together (but couldn't!), and made friends. Once Colin had got the hang of it, saying "Sorry" and talking about their differences seemed to work most of the time. And do you know what? His hump grew smaller and smaller until he felt as light and free as air!

Discussion points

- Why was Colin Camel's hump growing bigger? How do children who feel angry show their feelings?

- Colin Camel's first mum had a heavy hump. How does it make children feel when their parents are angry and upset a lot of the time?

- Colin kept kicking the other young camels. What was he afraid of?

- Do children in your school fall out? What about? Who helps them sort out their arguments? Can children solve their own arguments?

- What should parents do when children are having arguments?

- When should adults get involved and when should they not?

- How do you know when something is done on purpose or happens by accident? Do you put things right when you fall out? Does blame help or hinder?

- The mother camels had some young ones demonstrate how to sort out arguments. What works best? Do you have a scheme like this in your school? Do you know how you might sort out your next argument?

Activity

- Draw some camels with humps of different sizes onto card and cut them out. Re-enact the story above.

....

THEME: FROM POWERLESSNESS TO TRANSFORMATION

Source of problem

Egbert's story was written for a traumatised nine-year-old boy, Nathan, whose adoptive placement had disrupted. Part of the problem stemmed from his belief that the social worker had lost her way when she took him from his birth mother. His foster carer said that she "walked on eggshells" to avoid upsetting him.

The metaphor

Egbert's shell is described as 'hard yet fragile, easily cracked'. The egg's life begins in a noisy, smelly and overcrowded battery farm, a metaphor for the cramped and unhygienic accommodation in which the child had been raised. Traumatised children fear mockery and can find sophisticated humour hard to understand. To be able to share feelings and laughter is a step towards emotional reciprocity, So the story is gently humorous – the mother hen is described as "egg-sausted", a joke to be enjoyed for its simplicity.

Egbert never knows when or where his journey will end; his confusion parallels that of children taken from their birth families to new situations. For Egbert, the wait to be "chosen" felt interminable. Even when he is selected, Egbert suffers more nerve-wracking anxiety. At his new home, he is placed in the fridge (the coldness symbolising anxiety and fear). To convey a sense of hope, the story is given a happy outcome with the cooked egg being transformed into pancakes so delicious that it prompts the child, who relishes them, to train as a chef.

The story had resonance for Nathan who recognised that if change can be effected in a fiction with some realism (eggs change form on being cooked), it may also be possible in real life.

Egbert, the good egg!

Once upon a time there was an overcrowded chicken coop full of hens. As they jostled each other, feathers flew all over the smelly, noisy barn. One day, Henny Hen laid a perfectly formed egg, which she named Egbert. Henny was immensely proud, even though after laying she was quite exhausted, or shall we say "egg-sausted"!

She was sure that her egg would be chosen by the farmers, as it looked so perfect! She hoped it would be admired for its fine shape, but felt sad that she would not be allowed to raise Egbert as her chick, because she was in a battery farm where eggs are collected quickly before hatching. She knew that Egbert's shell was hard yet fragile, so would easily crack if it was not handled carefully.

Soon, Egbert was picked up by the farmer and put in a special basket with other well-formed eggs. They were taken in a rickety lorry to a factory and packed into boxes. Egbert was rattled and confused by the rapidly changing smells and temperature. He worried about where he'd finish up and what would happen to him. Egbert wanted to make his mother hen proud of him but was terrified of being crushed. Eventually he was placed on a shelf in a supermarket. People kept picking him up and putting him back as soon as they noticed that one of the other eggs had a slight crack. Egbert began to despair that he'd never be chosen but would sit there and rot.

After what felt like years, but was really just a few days, a customer took Egbert out and put him in another box with five perfect eggs. Egbert began to feel excited (egg-cited) as he was carried to the checkout. He cruised along the conveyer belt, was then put in a bag, carried to the car, driven to a new house and placed in the fridge! Egbert wondered what would happen next! He heard voices that seemed to be talking about eggs.

'We can use them to make sweet or savoury foods, such as pancakes and soufflés, cakes, meringues, omelettes, or we can fry, scramble or boil them,' said the mother as she took Egbert out of the fridge. Egbert felt dizzy with exhilaration (eggs-ileration)!

'The shell is hard!' said a child.

'Watch me crack it!' said Mum.

'It's runny!' said the child.

'Ahaa...that will change!' said Mum.

She mixed the egg with flour, sugar and milk and poured some into the hot pan. Soon it spread and thickened into a pancake. After a few minutes Mum told the child, 'It's set now!' She slid the pancake onto the plate and poured syrup over it. 'Yum! Delicious!' said the child, between mouthfuls. From inside the child's tummy, Egbert glowed with happiness. He was thinking to himself, 'My mother hen would be so proud!'

The child grew strong from eating good food. Because he was interested in how eggs and other foods change form during cooking, he became a chef, which just goes to show that you never know what great things can grow from small beginnings.

Discussion points

- Henny was proud of her egg but knew she couldn't hatch it. How do you think she felt? Do you know what a battery farm is? What do you think it would be like to be in one?

- Egbert's shell was hard, yet could crack easily. The journey to the supermarket was nerve-wracking. How did Egbert feel? Children can find it hard to cope with journeys. What might help them?

- Eggs are brought to supermarkets then chosen by the customers. Adopted children have been chosen by their adoptive parents. Do you think parents should be able to choose their children?

- Egbert waits ages to be chosen, as do children waiting to be adopted. What does the waiting feel like? What could help children while they are waiting?

- When they are cooked, eggs change shape and form. Can you think of other things that change form? How do they change?

Activity

- Think of all the ingredients you can put into an omelette or into cupcakes. You could then make one or the other. If you make cupcakes, you could decorate each one with a face with a particular expression.

> The stories above can help children to learn the language of feelings. When they feel released of self-blame and encouraged by their adoptive parents' expressed interest in them, creating stories with new preferred outcomes can raise children's self-esteem. In these stories, empathy and nurture are modelled by adult figures to convey that children can hope for a more rewarding future.

Using fairy stories to help children heal

This chapter shows how you can use traditional stories and myths in a way in which children and young people can draw courage to recover from the hurt of rejection and abuse. In the battle against ill fortune, the stoic heroes and heroines of these tales can inspire new hope in youngsters who, due to maltreatment, have grown up to believe that they did not deserve to exist.

The power of fairy tales

Stories represent the human condition. Themes of betrayal, deceit and rivalry, which typically preoccupy children in care, have, since time immemorial, proliferated in plays and stories that have entertained and educated us, including the myths of ancient Greece, the plays of Shakespeare, the stories of Charles Dickens and the fairy tales of Hans Christian Andersen and the Brothers Grimm.

While there is a wealth of contemporary literature for children, traditional fairy tales can carry a special significance for the fearful child. Although many of these tales have been "sanitised" by Disney, they still retain some of the archetypal symbols of the original versions. For instance, the evil stepmother or witch is an archetype that personifies maternal failure to care – *Hansel and Gretel* tells of two innocent children who demonstrate the capacity and courage to outwit the evil witch. The story of *The three little pigs* gives a sense of prediction that rebuilds neural pathways. As the eldest pig learns from the errors of his younger brothers how to build the safest house, the three pigs can be seen to represent the child at progressive developmental stages, while the wolf can be a symbol of the "bad self".

Children are highly dependent on parental love and approval. To sense that their sibling is preferred over them can leave the unfavoured child with a sense of inferiority and rejection. To affirm such a status, she may become a "Cinderella". But, in the fairy tale, as Bettelheim (1979) noted, Cinderella rises above her dejected state by her own efforts, and in so doing, gives readers the hope that someday their own "fairy godmother" might come.

Fairy tales invite children to explore thoughts and dreams and to find ways to overcome difficulties. Encouragement to take risks helps them to embrace the way forward rather than resist the future. Abuse and abandonment can leave children feeling overwhelmed with anger at their own impotence. In stories, many will identify with the hero's motivation to avenge wrongdoing without being scared of the consequences since, after all, it is "just a story". From seeing a connection between the character's difficulties and their own inner conflicts, the child is enticed by the hero's success to "keep trying".

Von Franz (1996) reflects that fairy tales celebrate the value of flexibility rather than rigid principles. In these traditional tales, the childlike qualities of innocence and trust are lauded in characters such as the princess, who unquestioningly kisses a frog before she knows that he will turn into a prince.

To young children, adults can seem like threatening giants, but stories like *Jack and the beanstalk* show that, with a little cunning, a child can acquire the power to get the better of grown-ups. By reading these stories to their children, parents convey their approval of such (fictional) retaliation. Even in fantasy, the feelings are legitimate and, although "unreal", are not untrue.

For very young children, traditional fables about animals have long proved effective to engage their interest. Children will listen intently to hear what the lion said to the mouse, as they relate to animal "characters" that bear human characteristics and feelings with which they are familiar. For this reason, in Chapter 2, several of the stories aimed at younger children depict animals as the main character. As Gersie and King (1990) observed, by triggering and nurturing the imagination, stories allow children to actualise their potential.

Which story to use?

In seeking stories that your child will find particularly inspiring, fairy tales provide a useful starting point as so many of them feature the themes of loss, betrayal, rivalry and of feeling demeaned or disregarded. For example, in *Jack and the beanstalk*, the child, dismissed by his mother, proves his worth by outwitting a giant, thereby giving a timid child confidence for dealing with people who intimidate him. *Beauty and the beast* is often chosen by children who have been sexually abused (as the beast represents the abuser), but it also features themes of betrayal versus loyalty and of ugliness versus beauty. *Goldilocks and the three bears* has a resonance for children who, having moved to a new family, are still trying to cope with the many changes and new faces in their life. A story that can be used to explore the wait to be rescued from abuse, or for a long promised "forever family", is *Sleeping Beauty*, in which a prince is needed to break the spell which wakes the princess from a hundred years of sleep. This story can also help a child who holds onto a fantasy of being rescued by her birth parents ('if only they knew where to find me!'). Similarly, for the purpose of exploring the loss of identity, which commonly affects children in care, *Anastasia* features a princess who escapes death and by finding her mother in another country, eventually discovers her true identity.

How to use the stories

Parents are advised to tell the story without offering (possibly unwelcome) connections to the child's own situation, in order that the child can enjoy it. The case examples throughout this book give ideas for expanding children's imagination in a way that will enable them to process their experience.

Children's interpretations of traditional tales

The stories that follow were developed by children who, having been inspired by the original version, related aspects of it to their own experience and adapted them accordingly. While children are often content to improvise, it adds to their enjoyment to have props that will support the story. These might include items such as teddy bears for *Goldilocks and the three bears*, a decorative jug to serve as Aladdin's magic lamp, and some paper plates on which to draw masks that can help to define the fictional role. Children can paint scenery and many will also enjoy making their own props for the play from simple craft materials, such as pieces of coloured card, newspaper, boxes and masking tape.

HARLEY: FEELING REJECTED

History

Harley, 13, was relinquished when he was six months old. His birth mother had felt isolated and depressed and decided she could not give her baby the love and care that he needed. Harley was then adopted by Mitchell and Jenny, who went on to have two more children but separated when Harley was seven. For the next four years Harley remained with his adoptive mother, who then demanded that his adoptive father take him. As his brothers remained with their mother, Harley felt terribly rejected. He never displayed anger but his "clowning" intensely irritated his father and stepmother, both high achievers who were impatient with Harley for being disorganised and barely scraping through at school. Harley was 12 when he learned from his adoptive parents that he was adopted. The shock made him yearn to find his birth parents.

Intervention

Over the course of ten sessions of dramatherapy, improvising scenes from his early life helped Harley to understand the circumstances of his adoption and to reconcile to his situation. He felt excluded from popular groups at school and picked on by his step-siblings. In the sessions, he drew androgynous caricatures, which he then dramatised. This led him to examine the personality traits of the characters he had created and to compare qualities he admired with those he despised. The story of Aladdin inspired Harley to enact the version that follows, using a story mat and toy figures of characters from the story.

Aladdin's adventures

by Harley, age 13

Once upon a time there was a poor unfortunate servant boy called Aladdin who had to steal to stay alive! He lived in a castle called Valagar with his pet owl, Nike. He wanted to get out more and find someone to love. As he walked to the market he saw a man wearing a black mask. Aladdin asked him, 'Do you have any transport?' The masked man replied, 'You can use my magic carpet but you must treat it well'. Aladdin said, 'That's crazy! There's no such thing!' But the carpet magically appeared and the man told him to take care of it.

The owl perched on the back and Aladdin sat at the front, asking, 'How do I make it go?' The man told him to say: 'Magic Carpet run away with me, far away to my destiny!' Aladdin repeated the words. He and his owl flew to places they'd never been before. They landed in the desert, jumped off and looked around. There was only blazing hot sun and mountains in the distance. They jumped back onto the carpet and Aladdin repeated the words.

They set off again and came to a place near a town. Aladdin got off and went into the town. He was thirsty and tried to steal water but there were lots of guards, so it was tricky. As he walked past them, he bumped into a beautiful girl called Jasmine. Clumsily, Aladdin knocked into her so she dropped her food and fell to the ground. He picked her up and said, 'Sorry!' She walked off but he ran to her and asked, 'Who are you?' But all she said is 'I'm not allowed out! I can't let anyone see me!' Aladdin told her, 'Step on my magic carpet!' Jasmine said, 'Don't be silly!' but he promised to prove that it worked. They set off to her castle. 'This is a lovely place! Are you really a princess?' asked Aladdin. Jasmine introduced Aladdin to the Sultan, who said, 'Daughter, you need a husband!' He turned to Aladdin and asked, 'Do you want to marry her?' Jasmine said, 'I'm not ready yet!' Her father said, 'You are only allowed to love one man' and told Aladdin, 'You can marry her if you find the magic lamp'.

Aladdin went to search for the lamp. In the forest he heard a rustle. Suddenly, there before him was a wizard, a blue monster and a wrestler. Scared, Aladdin explained, 'I'm only looking for a magic lamp!' The fearsome three said, 'We'll fight you!' Swiftly, Aladdin phoned Nike. The owl arrived to help, flew into the monster's face and pecked his eyes out. Aladdin asked Nike to help him find the magic lamp. Nike said, 'OK. So long as I get a share of any riches you find!' They shook hands on the deal and set off to the jungle. The owl told Aladdin to go to the snake, who was polishing the lamp. They found the snake and said, 'We need the lamp desperately!' Owl spoke in snake language and persuaded the snake to let them have it on one condition. 'Bring me the sand of all eternity!' Nike said, 'OK! My father's got it', and sped off, soon returning with the sand that he exchanged for the lamp. Aladdin and his friends flew to Zanzibar where the Sultan lived. He said, 'You may marry my daughter tomorrow!' It was a big rush. Aladdin wanted all his friends to come. The night before the wedding they had a party. Afterwards, they staggered home drunk. The next day, Aladdin and Jasmine got married. They set up home in Zanzibar and lived happily ever after.

How the story helped

From enacting his version of the traditional story, Harley experienced the good fortune of having friends who helped him to achieve his goal. His story features 'a poor unfortunate boy who had to steal to stay alive'. The hero encounters dangers but the rewards reaped by his staying power helped Harley to realise that he too had skills and courage that had helped him to survive. Encouraged, he drew up several advice sheets to remind him of how to cope with challenging situations.

Activity

● Paint a picture of a genie – make three wishes – what happens?

NAOMI: DEALING WITH ANXIETY

History

Naomi and her brothers had been removed to foster care following domestic violence and neglect. Naomi's parents had themselves suffered abusive childhoods and had been in and out of local authority care. Both drank heavily. Naomi's father was 30 years older than their mother, who left him and went on to have several more partners. Their mother was alternately coercive or helpless, and unresponsive to her children's emotional needs. Naomi swung between heightening and inhibiting her feelings. She would scream for hours when her will was thwarted and intimidated the younger children whom she set up to be blamed for her misdemeanours. At other times, Naomi was submissive, wary of intimacy, appearing invulnerable. Now aged eight and about to be placed for adoption, she expressed her anxieties through play.

Intervention

Naomi loved dressing up to enact familiar stories, in particular, *The three little pigs*, in which she had the errant Wolf's tail "burned" in the fire. Although Wolf (therapist) apologised for hurting the pigs, the Pig (Naomi) was not convinced. Debating how a betrayed creature might learn to trust prompted her to give Wolf another chance: 'Do you want to make friends?' When a donkey (therapist) owned up to being bullied, Naomi made "magic spells" to ensure its survival. In another session, her version of the Snow White story evolved.

Snow White gets tired out!
By Naomi, age 8

Once upon a time there was a vain, proud Queen who ruled the land. Her daughter, Snow White, grew up to be very beautiful. One day, as she looked at her reflection, the Queen asked, 'Mirror, mirror on the wall, who is the fairest one of all?' The mirror replied, 'Snow White!' Scared, Snow White hid under her bed, fell asleep and woke up shocked to find the Queen telling her to go into the forest or be killed by soldiers. Snow White ran, followed by rabbits, reindeer and turtles trying to save her.

Hours later, she came to a house in the forest. On entering, she saw that it was very messy, so she started to tidy up. Snow White was very tired after all that running and cleaning, so was fast asleep when the dwarves came home. 'Oh look, our house is tidy!' they said. Hearing them, Snow White woke up feeling very scared. They asked, 'What's your name?' Snow White told them and explained why she ran away from home. The dwarves said, 'Would you like to live with us?' She replied, 'Yes please!' They cooked her favourite food – sausages, chips and beans, with orange squash, followed by chocolate chip ice cream. By now, Snow White was so tired that she fell asleep before they finished cooking, but woke up to eat it. The dwarves gave her a string puppet called Pink Teddy. She learned how to make it walk and run. It turned out that Pink Teddy had escaped from a cruel puppet master. Snow White knew how that felt!

The next day, the dwarves left for work, warning Snow White not to answer the door. But on hearing a knock, she forgot their warning and opened it. A witch said, 'I have some fine rosy apples! Would you like to try some?' Snow White took one. 'They are delicious!' said the Witch. Snow White bit into the apple and fell to the floor in a deep sleep. Cackling, the witch left. When the dwarves came home they were shocked to find their princess lying as if dead. They could not wake her. One of the dwarves phoned a newspaper to tell them what happened, asking, 'Can you write about it in case anyone can help her?'

A few years later, a handsome prince came across some old newspapers and read about Snow White. Quickly, he mounted his horse and galloped off to find her. 'Thank goodness!' said the dwarves when he arrived. They led him to Snow White. The Prince said, 'I'm so upset! The Queen has really hurt her!' By now, assuming she was dead, the dwarves had placed Snow White in a coffin. The

Prince kissed Snow White and she woke up. He asked her, 'Will you marry me?' Snow White said, 'Yes!'

They married and had three dogs and three children. They loved to eat lasagne, cheese, scrambled egg, bacon, sausage, beans and tomatoes. The children's favourite toy was a puppet that Snow White used to play with when she came to live with the dwarves. At times she still fell down and lay as if dead. 'Oh my poor girl!' said the Prince. But she got up, saying 'Only joking!' They lived happily ever after.

. . . .

How the story helped

Naomi had been reluctant to admit her worries, but her stories revealed her anxiety about moving to her new adoptive family. Like Naomi, Pink Teddy had been 'badly treated by its master.' Collapsing into sleep allowed Naomi as Snow White/Princess to express her need to retreat from stress that she anticipated but could not verbalise. Reviving, she would say 'Only joking' in the manner of a child used to appeasing adults. Naomi checked that every detail of her version had been recorded, keen to ensure that her puppeteer skills had also been included. Giving Snow White's pets the names of her adoptive family's dogs provided the link that helped her acknowledge her real fears. Having her feelings validated and receiving reassurance through fictional privacy enabled Naomi to make a satisfactory move to adoption.

Activity

● Make seven dwarves from card. Decide who they can help next.

. . . .

CANDY: FEELING "EVIL"

History

Eight-year-old Candy and her six-year-old sister were waiting to be placed together for adoption. Candy's relationship with her younger sister was fragile, but in the foster home they had begun to tolerate each other and play well together. Although they were sisters, their care histories were very different. Candy had lived with her mother for her first five years and witnessed considerable violence. Her younger sister had been accommodated from infancy in multiple foster placements between brief returns home. While her sister was less demanding and more distant to the carer, Candy, although highly insecure, quickly attached to her foster mother, perhaps relieved to be safe. The move to adoption revived her anxieties. Candy feared that she was a nasty person and that no one would want her if they knew how bad she was.

Intervention

Candy drew inspiration from fairy stories and the various costumes in the dressing up bag to explore her feelings in dramatic play and instinctively connected to the story of Cinderella. She took the role of stepmother, casting her foster mother as the ugly sister and the therapist as Cinderella. The adults followed Candy's direction, using their own feelings to mirror the effects of ill treatment at the hands of the stepmother, but also to offer alternative ways to deal with situations in order to communicate the benefits of more desirable approaches.

Cinderella's bad luck

By Candy, age 7

The ill-tempered stepmother set her children against each other. She told Cinderella to send her sister to her room. Cinderella protested but the stepmother shouted, 'Don't give me lip!' and banished her to her bedroom. Cinderella spent lots of time locked in her room. At other times she was given nasty jobs and complained bitterly. 'You want me out of the way! You're angry! I feel useless!' Vengefully, her stepmother yelled: 'Shut up! You do everything wrong! You're a stupid idiot!' The stepmother continued to be horrible to her children.

Cinderella's ugly sister wondered if her mother would ever be kind. She said, 'You want a nice daughter but I need a mother to tell me what to do. Can you show me how to be nice?' The stepmother looked unsure. The ugly sister explained that she wanted a mother who would cook nice dinners and talk to her in a kind voice. The stepmother listened carefully. She decided to take her daughters to a café where they had dinner. When they came home she let them choose a holiday.

How the story helped

The play allowed Candy to admit her fears about adoption. Her foster carer acknowledged that it would be hard for Candy to learn to trust more strangers, but encouraged her to look forward to her life with these new parents. So Candy was feeling hopeful as the introductions began. Sadly, the adoptive parents had no prior experience of dealing with sibling rivalry which quickly reignited. They rejected Candy and kept her sister. Fortunately, Candy returned to her foster carer, who later adopted her, and both children adjusted well.

Activity

- Create a clay model of Cinderella – ask her what she hopes for.

Myths and legends

There are a multitude of stories in which heroes conquer adversity. Their potency invokes images of power and prowess. These stories stimulate the imagination and enhance children's problem-solving skills by conveying the message that they can achieve their ambitions: 'I am, therefore I can!'

IVAN: DISTURBING DREAMS

History
Ivan, aged 11, had been brought up by abusive grandparents. His mother had left the family and his father had died of a drug overdose. Ivan had been in two foster placements prior to his current long-term placement. A fearful child, his repeated nightmares of earlier abuse were causing loss of sleep and appetite, which was making it difficult for him to attach to his new carers.

Intervention
Ivan was inspired by tales from Greek mythology. He loved dressing up and constructing his own versions of *The Odyssey* and *Jason and the golden fleece*, into which he wove modern day heroes, Ali G and Jackie Chan. In his role as Hercules, Ivan displayed determination to overpower the monsters, which represented his earlier abuse and which had been plaguing him in his dreams. Dramatic play that exercised his imagination enabled Ivan to annihilate the monsters with the help of his "friends".

Jason slays the dragon
by Ivan, age 11

This is the story of Jason, a mighty and powerful hero. In the land where he lived, there was a dragon with five arms, 16 legs and 10 heads. Whenever you killed one head, it popped up again. The dragon didn't die but killed you instead!

Jason told the dragon, 'I will kill you!' Trying to slay it, he said to his friend, 'Monkey, I need help!' Monkey had a magic jewel in his head. The jewel lit up and burned the dragon's eye. Jason went back to fight the dragon but fell as if he was dead. Monkey stabbed the dragon and his diamond entered the dragon's body, then it entered Jasons' body as well. Transformed, Jason (now as Jackie Chan) performed one trick after another. As everyone watched the reincarnation of Jackie Chan, Ali G came and tried to trick the dragon. Jackie Chan used his magic hands and turned back into Jason. So in the end, it was Jason who killed the dragon.

How the story helped

Ivan was encouraged to explore the reason for each character's demeanour, as he directed the story of his experience of having been bullied, abused, mocked, demonised and forced to perform tricks, petrified of his abuser's highly unpredictable temper. Alternating roles as monster and hero led Ivan to recognise that he had adopted many guises in order to survive. He began to appreciate his own qualities of courage and stoicism. Creating magical solutions helped Ivan to discover that he had choices and could use the same skills in real life that he had used to effect transformation in these stories.

Activities

- Make swords from reinforced card and add a jewel (cellophane or small glass bead).

- Design a sword dance to use as a practice to prepare for battle.

Modern stories

Milo and the magic stones is a story by Marcus Pfeifer about a mouse who finds magical stones that bring light and warmth to his cave. The story has two endings. The "unhappy" ending (best read first) describes greedy mice taking too many stones, thereby causing the island to collapse. In the "happy" ending, mice replace the stones and the island is secure. Comparing the two outcomes is an effective way to show how the choices we make can affect our future, especially once the children appear ready to reconcile to earlier loss and rebuild their identity.

KEVIN: CLINGING TO INDEPENDENCE

History

Kevin, aged nine, and his younger brother, six, were adopted from foster care, having been severely neglected by their learning disabled parents. Kevin had been used to looking out for himself and his brother. He was determined to maintain his independence, so rejected his adoptive parent's attempts to help him with anything and everything. He also felt responsible for his younger brother and would try to take over parenting tasks. Kevin viewed himself as a "soldier" fighting a battle and felt compelled to keep his troops safe.

Intervention

Kevin was given ten sessions of therapy to help him make sense of the reasons for his removal from his birth family and the move to his adoptive family. Playing out the events of his history on a life map led Kevin to dramatise his early memories, in fictional contexts. In the eighth week, he was presented with the story, *Milo and the magic stones,* and some clay for the activity to follow. By this time, Kevin appeared ready to begin to attach to his adoptive parents.

After listening to the story of Milo and the magic stones, Kevin built a clay island on which he developed his own story. He allowed his mother to make the clay mice but spurned her ideas for providing food or shelter. Kevin's story projected the mice as isolated creatures who displayed no sign of enjoying comfort or pleasure. On hearing his mother and therapist wonder how these mice might survive, and what would make them feel safe and comfortable so that their life could be rewarding, Kevin constructed a wall to keep out intruders. He decided that his teddy also needed to be safe. Over the following weeks, Kevin used cardboard boxes and cartons to build a house (a possible symbol for building the future) for Teddy, planning around Teddy's needs (which, of course, represented his own). He built two storeys, a staircase, a banister (to prevent accidents), a larder, a bed and a garage. Significantly, Kevin made a friend for Teddy and began to accept his mother's help with building and finding the pieces he needed.

How the story helped

Kevin was enabled to address his needs by projecting them onto the mice in his clay tableau and then his teddy from his first family, a "transitional object" (Winnicot, 1971) that gave him comfort. His adoptive mother's engagement in his play helped Kevin to begin to attach securely for the first time in his life.

REBECCA: SURVIVOR, NOT VICTIM

History

Rebecca, aged 11, had been physically, sexually and emotionally abused in her family of origin. Having moved back and forth between parents in different countries, she was taken into care when she was seven years old and had lived in 12 different foster placements. At her request, Rebecca had been separated from her sisters. In her new long-term placement, she expressed anger towards her father and refused to acknowledge photos of her parents. Four years behind in learning, and presenting as sad and dejected, Rebecca struggled to explain her feelings.

Intervention

Rebecca had little confidence in her abilities and was afraid to engage in activities that required imagination. At the start of therapy, she played card games suited to preschool age, until, being encouraged to experiment with clay and paint led her to make models of a brave dog and a scared rabbit. As they seemed to represent aspects of Rebecca's personality, the therapist constructed a story about these two characters, which helped Rebecca to accept her history and inspired her to create her own stories from images in her artwork. Hearing tales of magic and transformation fired her enthusiasm for dramatic play and she enjoyed dressing up and making her own props. Rebecca began to see that the decisions taken by characters in stories affected their outcome. In leading her to believe in her own volition, *The Wizard of Oz* proved to have a compelling influence.

Think for yourself!

Rebecca took the lead role of Dorothy and directed her therapist and foster mother to be Tin Man, Lion, and Scarecrow. The friends escaped from the witch but became stuck in their hiding places. While it was important to move according to Rebecca's direction, when she was stuck, she needed help to extricate herself. Tin Man (therapist) protested that if they kept hiding, they would never manage to find the Wizard. The friends made a plan to creep up on the witch and frighten her by shouting in unison. Thrilled at the sense of power this gave her, Rebecca declared that the plan had worked.

Taking the role of Wizard, she then directed her friends to go to the palace and queue to make their requests: Dorothy wanted to get home; Tin Man desired a heart; Lion wanted courage; and Scarecrow a brain. Requiring minimal prompting, Rebecca as the Wizard told each in turn that they already had the qualities they needed: 'It's all in your hands – you just have to think for yourself!'

How the story helped

In playing out this story, Rebecca discovered the thrill of friendship and the power of the group for saying "No" to bullies. Acting as Wizard, she realised that she understood the message of the story and that not only was she able to make decisions for herself but that her decisions affected the way others related to her and she to them. Involving her foster carer in the play also helped to secure her placement. The foster carer supported Rebecca in reconstructing her identity as a survivor rather than as a victim. Creative activity led Rebecca to choreographing dance moves and "shows" for her foster family. She went on to act out many more stories and to construct her own.

> Children who lack the confidence to explain their fears verbally tend to express them spontaneously through their fictional characters. The safety of fiction allows the child to explore how the undesired aspects of self are experienced by others. Effecting desired outcomes enables children to find that their strengths invariably outweigh their weaknesses.
>
> The imaginative exploration of traditional and contemporary stories stimulates creative activity.

Using drama for recovery

5

We experience and express feelings and sensations long before we learn to use words. Therefore children are able to make more sense of what has happened to them by physically re-enacting their early history than from verbal explanations alone. Research has long established the effectiveness of dramatic play for supporting children's development (Russ, 2004; Russ and Niec, 2011).

Reworking their history through drama allows children to disentangle and put right the mistaken assumptions that often lead them to blame themselves for their rejection. This chapter provides scripts drawn from children's life histories, while the next one illustrates the dramatic application of imaginary scenarios in which children can explore their experience in a safe way. These scenarios facilitate the achievement of goals that children may have previously dismissed as out of their reach.

The "Theatre of Attachment" model

A method for helping children to explore their troubling memories is described and illustrated by scripts from my "Theatre of Attachment" practice. This is based on the following principles:

- Adoptive and foster placements can be secured by improving mutual understanding between parents and children, from joint engagement (Dance and Rushton, 2005).

- Children's resilience is enhanced when they realise that their adoptive parents know about what happened to them, and that as choices had been available to their birth parents, they need not blame themselves for what happened.

- The use of stories, drama and play is effective for developing a positive and affective relationship, enabling greater emotional closeness.

- Attunement develops from inter-subjective experience (Hughes, 2006) and is enhanced by sensory play (Jennings, 2011).

- Therapeutic work in the family's home facilitates play, learning from which is more easily transferred to everyday situations. Many adoptive parents and foster carers prefer this.

- Parents who understand the impact of trauma appreciate the effect of their child's past experience. This helps them to view their child's behaviour as a mechanism for survival, rather than as a personal attack.

Dramatising life history

Children who have suffered loss and trauma, including neglect, are often stuck in the present, unable to think about either their past or the future. Dramatic play allows them to process their experience of loss and rework their trauma so that they are able to anticipate and plan for a more hopeful future.

Increasingly, there are new ways of sharing information that can impact on children and young people who use social networking websites such as Facebook. Many children yearn to find their birth relatives and many birth parents want to make contact with their children. Easy access to social networking sites has rendered attempts at confidentiality less effective for protecting vulnerable children. Many looked after or adopted children are not aware of their full history. Explaining what led to their removal from their birth family will help to avert the risk and shock of unwelcome disclosures and possible exploitation and keep children safe.

However, providing information in a language that children are too young, learning disadvantaged, or too anxious to absorb, or giving insufficient detail for them to fully understand their history, is to risk their becoming further traumatised. Traumatised children tend to be especially resistant to hearing about their life history, fearing that 'if they know why I was rejected they'll abandon me again!' Yet if children are unable to express fears based on incorrect assumptions about their past, the risk of longer-term mental ill health, built on self-loathing, increases.

Life history plays are a series of brief "snapshots" of events that culminate in a reassuring ending that will reduce the fears that many children find difficult to admit. Many older children and young people benefit from participating in, or watching, such a play, but to begin this process, emotionally fragile children may feel safer with a story such as *The elephant who felt different* in Chapter 2. Indeed, younger children often find that talking to a puppet is much easier than talking directly to an adult, and glove puppets can be used to good effect to stimulate conversations as in the example below.

Example

Parent *(holding puppet called Henry):*
 Henry has noticed you look sad today!
Child: I'm just thinking! That's all.
Parent: Can you tell Henry about it? He wants to help!
Child: It's my old mummy. It's her birthday today!
Parent *(has the puppet whisper in her ear):*
 Henry says he feels terrible. He knows how bad it must feel, missing your
 mummy. You must be wishing you could see her and give her a birthday present!
Child: Yeah, if only I could. But she's dead. She got ill. You know that!
Parent *(using Henry's voice):*
 I wish I knew more about that. Can you tell me?
Child: It's a very long story!
Parent *(as Henry):*
 I've got all the time in the world. Please tell me!
The child describes how his mother became ill and died and how lonely he felt. The parent uses reflective listening skills – listening attentively and relaying their understanding of what the child has said back to the child (see Corrigan and Moore, 2011).

Other ways to use puppets

- "Wise Owl" suggests comforting ways to help children to sleep

- A "parrot" gives advice on hygiene (see example in Chapter 6)

- A "streetwise" character can advise on how to cope with bullying

- A brave "lion" explains why anger needs to be controlled

- A "princess" discusses eating problems and considers new ways to enhance her image that win approval and a sense of self-control

How best to help traumatised children is a controversial issue as we always, rightly, worry about making things worse. Yet, for them, the risk of remaining a "victim" means having a lack of control over their life, a predicament described by Verrier (2003, p.108) as being like 'flotsam on the sea – floating with the tide, having no rudder to allow for direction or purpose'. Van der Kolk *et al* (2007) advise that, provided the child is safe, the repeated reworking of traumatic memories from which new interpretations can be made reduces the extremity of the pain. Of course, learning specific facts can reignite anxiety and care must be taken to avoid causing shame or embarrassment to the child.

From observing coping mechanisms adopted by traumatised children, Lahad (2000) has developed a strengths-based narrative approach to enhance interaction. He advocates the use of drama, incorporating music and textures. Sensory experience is absorbed by the most primitive parts of the brain which prompt fight–flight–freeze responses. Combining these sensory experiences with a reconstruction of previously frightening events in a way that reframes the child's experiences as being one of heroic survival builds new connections between these lower parts of the brain and the higher reasoning cortex where ordinary memory is stored, thus enabling traumatic memory to be processed safely.

The power of drama

Drama can arouse powerful emotions so parents need to be ready to deal with the impact of unforeseen triggers. For example, the sight of dolls reminded one child of terrorising trauma in her infancy, while another young person howled in pain as the play about his life history began.

Guidance for parents

Foster carers and adoptive parents who are seeking specialist help for their children may wish to consider the following issues:

- Do the children have any awareness of why they are in care?
- Do they appear to blame themselves? If so:
  - Are they anxious about why they are adopted or fostered?
- Are they willing to talk about their birth parents? If not:
  - Do they suffer problems that indicate unresolved issues such as sleeplessness, enuresis, soiling, stealing or aggression?
- Do the children overreact to seemingly harmless stimuli with "fight, flight or freeze" responses, thus revealing the impact of past trauma?

The more deeply troubled children will need to be referred for therapy involving play and drama in which inclusion of parents could be very useful.

Adoptive parents and long-term foster carers have the right to see and retain copies of documents that detail the children's history and the care decisions taken on their behalf. This information can be used to reassure the child that they are not to blame for what happened to them and that their story can lead to a "happy ending". If facts are discussed openly, children will not worry that information is being kept from them. It is most important to ensure that information is given sensitively and that the children and young people are emotionally supported in the process that follows. Corrigan and Moore (2011) advise on how to explain complex issues about a child's circumstances, such as parents' mental illness, rape, imprisonment, substance addiction, sexual abuse and learning disability, as do Morrison (2012) and Wolfs (2009, 2010).

Getting help

For some children, being taken away from their parents feels like a kidnap. They may continue to believe that they should be with their birth parents and deny the abuse they suffered. Children who have lived without boundaries may "spill out" personal information indiscriminately, being unaware of the risks. Adoptive parents and foster carers often feel blamed for what went wrong in the child's early life. For this reason, it can be beneficial to involve a third party for whom the child's history does not have the emotional connotations that it has for adoptive parents. Obtaining professional support is recommended, but if it cannot be accessed, relatives or close friends may be able to help. They will need to know some of the background, be involved in planning, and may then take part in the drama or sit with the child to reassure them during the performance.

While the end goal is to enable children to view themselves as "heroes" rather than "victims", it is important to convey where birth parents wanted to love their children and tried to care for them, and that the children are not responsible for adverse circumstances. In my experience, adults who engage in this process gain greater appreciation of the degree to which birth parents were affected by stress factors. This insight can help them to explain with greater empathy the complexity of decisions that led to the children being placed in care.

Parents need to understand the difficulties that stem from neurological damage that can delay emotional and social development (Perry and Szalavitz 2006; Schore 2006). Empathy is necessary for the development of conscience for children to understand "right" and "wrong". The scripts that follow provide examples of processing the information detailing these children's past experiences.

Preparation

Prior to engaging children in the plays about their life history, it is helpful to prepare them via exercises that stimulate their senses and imagination, and warm up their voice and body.

Warm-up exercises

- From cards, magazines or newspapers, assemble pictures of people and create a sequence of events that develop into a story featuring a hero, friend, adventure, problem, solution, and what happens next.

- Animal puppets can introduce their "character", who might ask, 'Are people afraid of you?' or 'Are you afraid of people?'

- Mime: pass round an imaginary object, like a knife, kitten, old wallet, expensive necklace, hot potato, miming how the object is handled. Whoever guesses the object correctly takes the next turn.

- In pairs, each person acts as if watching an emotionally stirring event such as an exciting football match, a lorry colliding with a car, a baby crying, a rat running over their feet, or a wild animal on the loose.

- Each person takes a turn miming their reaction to sounds like a bomb explosion, a favourite tune, thunder, doorbell, aeroplane, news just heard.

- Provide a variety of smells from a flower, herbs, an onion, TCP, burnt toast, perfume. Share reactions and imagine a setting for something pleasant or horrible to happen. Decide on the outcome and improvise the scene.

- Encourage the child to taste fruits and raw vegetables, suck a drink through a straw, lick ice cream, pop balloons and blow whistles.

- Invite the child to select pieces of fabric of varying texture that they like and say which aspect of their personality it represents: tough, delicate, sparkly, straight, soft, and so on. Discuss the feelings each arouses.

See Corrigan and Moore (2011) for further ideas to prepare for the role.

Structure

Prior to enacting the life history, children will need to know the main facts of their story, which, for younger and less able children, can be conveyed by playing out the events on a life map with simple drawings of the houses in which they lived, and using toys to represent people in their life (see Corrigan and Moore, 2011 for descriptions of life history maps).

There are several ways for children to participate in the drama of their life history, depending on their age, developmental stage and personality. They might draw posters and tickets, make props, or take charge of the music. Some prefer just to watch. Others are keen to act or may join in part of the way through. Afterwards, children can ask the "birth parent" why they took the decisions they did and adoptive parents or foster carers can describe how life would have been if the child had been born to them, and propose ways to nurture them.

Scripts

Scripts (based on the child's life history) provide a defined structure that protects children from being "carried away", becoming "unreal" or over-controlling. A play with a beginning, middle and end reduces lengthy periods to a brief time frame. To contextualise birth parents' circumstances, pre-written scripts are given a conversational style that invites a range of emotional expression likely to include humour, frustration, thrill, anger and being unresponsive.

The plays seek not to sensationalise, but to present brief "snapshots" of past events. In plays by the early Greeks, the messengers or chorus on stage described the worst excesses that occurred (offstage), leaving the audience to imagine the event (Jennings, 2011). Accordingly, to reduce the risk of overexciting or re-traumatising children, scenes from their history portray the aftermath, rather than actual incidents of violence or abuse. A key aim is to illustrate the pressures that led birth parents to act as they did. The plays have about 10 scenes, last around 20 to 30 minutes, and are followed by questions.

Improvisation

Improvisation gives children scope to develop the play in their own way, by reconstructing scenes to show what they would prefer to have happened. For this purpose, it will help to have a list of scenes to refer to. Older children and young people can be engaged in planning these in advance.

Children need parents to be authentic in their portrayal of roles. Dressing up invites laughter, which facilitates relaxation and is a useful defence against anxiety. During the play, adults can ask the child for direction: 'How do you want me to be?' Parents can speak as if they were the child: 'I'm scared I won't be very good', and perhaps ask: 'How do I know if I can trust this person? What do you think I should do?' Children like being consulted and will generally give advice. (Chapter 1 gives further guidance on managing complex feelings and behaviour that may arise in such play.)

Setting the scene

On the day, prepare scripts, dressing-up clothes and props. Clothing, hats and props help children to assume the posture and character of their role. Have a CD or mp3 player for music of the period, to evoke memories and emotions. Sound effects, music and props can lend a thrill and authenticity to the drama. Children can choose songs that their birth parents liked, or that they associate with previous placements. Younger children can make items out of card or paper, such as an axe, samurai sword, or cigarettes, that remind them of their earlier life.

Suggested items of clothing

A policeman's helmet
A judge's wig
A nurse's cap
A school shirt and tie
A baseball cap, scarves

Useful accessories and equipment

A stethoscope and phone
A baby blanket
A retractable (plastic) knife
A strip of paper rolled up to look like a cigarette
A black bin liner filled with clothes
A small bag of salt (symbolising drugs)

A case or bag on wheels, for house moving scenes
Life-sized baby dolls and dolls to represent other children

In the part of the room that will be used as the "stage", it is helpful to have a soft chair for scenes in which the birth mother can "give birth", also for the scenes that take place "at home". For scenes that involve a fight or attack, the "injured person" will need somewhere safe and comfortable to "fall".

TOM AND AARON'S STORY OF TRAUMA

History

Tom, aged seven, and Aaron, aged five, had been placed for adoption a year ago. Tom was having nightmares. At school, he feared children whose appearance triggered memories of past abuse. His mentally unstable parents had been involved in paedophilia. Tom believed that he did not deserve to be loved and was profoundly jealous of his younger brother.

The play

The adoptive parents and grandmother took part in this play while the children watched with their adoptive grandfather. Sometimes, plays begin with a scene from the birth parent's childhood to show how problems early in life affected them in adulthood, but in this case, due to the sheer scale and complexity of the history, it was decided to simplify it by opening the play with Tom's birth.

Scene 2 reveals that the children's birth mother, Debbie, has been injured by her partner and is feeling persecuted by the social worker. Meanwhile, the social worker tries to assert her authority but feels increasingly ineffectual in the face of Debbie's outrage. By the time Aaron is born, the father has left the family. The older children are taken into foster care but are soon returned to their mother, until, in Scene 4, we learn that social workers have decided that the risks for the children of remaining at home are too high. Scene 5 has the adoptive parents seeking children to complete their family, and in Scene 6, they meet Tom and Aaron. At the end, the children's birth mother, Debbie, returns to the stage to answer (prepared) questions.

Safe at last!

Scene 1: At hospital. Nurse hands baby Tom to his mum, Debbie.

Nurse: Here Debbie, take good care of him! You'll need your money now!

Debbie *(angrily):* What do you mean? Their dad's who you should be talking to!

Nurse: Well, he's saying you spend it all in the slot machines!

Debbie *(exploding into a coughing fit):*
What a cheek! It's him who drinks all our money away, not me! You've seen the state he gets in!

Nurse: There! There! *(she mops up)* I'll take baby. You have a nice little nap!

A short while later, Debbie picks up her baby. But he cries and she drops him.

Scene 2: At home. Social worker bangs on door then pushes it open.

Social worker: Hello, Debbie, you OK? Heard the police were round. Look at the state of you! Are the children all right? Come here Tom! Let me have a look!

Debbie: Don't bother to let me get a word in, will you? Jamie got a bit drunk last night. You ain't worried about me, just them kids you're checking up on!

Social worker: Debbie, I do worry about you! You can't keep letting Jamie hurt you! Look, I can arrange for you to go to a refuge. At least you'd be safe there!

Debbie: Nah! He'd only find me! Anyhow he's their father – he needs 'em.

Social worker: Sure, but they don't need him! Children need a proper home, hot dinners and clean clothes. They're never going to be safe with Jamie around!

Debbie *(shouts):* All right! I'll lock the doors 'n tell the police if he comes here.

Social worker: I wish you'd stop shouting, Debbie. I'm just trying to help! Think about your children! Tom's nappy's dirty. You must have left him like that for hours!

Debbie: Get lost! Just get out of my house, you and your preachy ways!

Scene 3: Children go to foster carers. Debbie is in hospital, having Aaron.

Foster carer: Hello Tom, goodness, I'm going to have my hands full now, aren't I!

Social worker: You did say you could manage until Debbie's due out of hospital.

Scene 4: At home. Social worker calls round.

Social worker: Debbie, I've some bad news! You know we had that big meeting when it was agreed that the kids' names had to go on a register?

Debbie: Yeah, so what?

Social worker: Well, we've had to go to court. We're worried the children aren't safe here, Debbie. We're asking the court to decide what happens.

Debbie *(screams):* Get out! I'm not putting up with this. I'll get my solicitor. He'll sort you out! *(She grabs knife – points it at social worker who backs out hurriedly.)*

Scene 5: At the Social Services office.

Adoptive parents walk round the room and look at the "children" (dolls), commenting, 'All these children need parents. I wish we could look after them.'
Then they see Tom and Aaron.

Adoptive mum: Ah, look at Tom and Aaron! They've got beautiful eyes and such cute little dimples! They're the right age, they'd be perfect for us!

Scene 6: Social worker introduces the children to the adoptive parents.

Social worker: This is Tom and Aaron. Tom's been ever so brave. He's waited a long time for this.

Adoptive parents: And we've waited a long time to adopt Tom and Aaron.

(Adoptive parents rock dolls and make baby talk. Debbie returns to the stage.)

Debbie: Oh, so is that how you do it? I'm so glad they've got you to look after them. I know you'll do a much better job than me.

The children ask her why she'd been unable to care safely for them. Debbie answers their questions and says she wishes she had been a better mother.

The children's response

Tom reeled at the sight of the "baby" (doll) dropped by Debbie in Scene 1. His memories of abuse flooded back but the play helped him to piece together the incidents of violence between his parents and their acquaintances. Aaron had many questions to ask his birth mother about why she had let them down. Placed at 18 months, he was shocked to find out that he had not been born to his adoptive mother who had never found a way to tell him that he had been adopted.

In the improvised play that followed, babies were "stolen" by pirates, then rescued and given nurturing attention by Tom and Aaron, as "parents".

Re-enactment of the children's history using water to symbolise love that flows from a jug to a glass until blocked by pain (represented by clingfilm stretched over the glass) (Corrigan and Moore, 2011) enabled Aaron to work out his anger and resume his affectionate relationship with his adoptive mother. Both children enjoyed playing as "babies" and painting hero pictures.

LIVING WITH SCHIZOPHRENIA: JANE'S STORY

History

Jane's mother, Cherelle, had schizophrenia and had been abused as a child. Cherelle's mother had also been brought up in a context of violence and abuse. Jane was sexually abused by her older brother. He lived with his grandmother but often visited his sister and brothers. Cherelle's health deteriorated. At her request, her sons were removed from her care. They went first to their grandmother then to foster care. Jane remained with her mother for two years but was never allowed to play outside because her mother feared she would be kidnapped. Jane often heard Cherelle talking with people when no one was there, but her most frightening experiences were of seeing her mother slash her wrists and having fits. At age nine, Jane was taken to foster care. She loved her mother, worried about her and desperately wished she could return to live with her.

The play

Therapy was arranged to help Jane adjust to the plan for long-term foster care. She read her history, which explained the reasons for her coming into care. The following script is from an improvisation led by Jane who took the part of Cherelle (and later, the judge). Jane cast her therapist and foster carer in the roles of Nan, the social worker, police officer, and Mum's partners. Much of the drama centred on the relationship between Cherelle and Jane's Nan, whom they experienced as domineering, callous and vindictive. The play enabled Jane to realise that Cherelle had never had any positive sense of self.

Why me?

Scene 1: At home.

Cherelle is curled up on the sofa. Her baby son tries to get her attention but she pushes him away. The door bell rings and a social worker enters.

Social worker: Hello Cherelle! How is baby Alex?
(Cherelle is silent. Baby cries. Social worker picks him up.)

Social worker: Alex wants you! Why don't you give him a cuddle?
Cherelle: *(shrugs)* Don't feel like it!
The door bell rings again. Nan arrives.

Nan: *(To social worker)*
           What are you doing here? How's my little grandson? Why's he crying?
           (Turns to Cherelle) You're a waste of space, Cherelle! Let me have him. I'll look after him!
Social worker: What do you think, Cherelle?
Cherelle: How should I know? Go on then! Take him! All she ever does is have a go at me!
Nan: Because you're useless, you can't look after yourself, let alone a baby!
Cherelle: You're so foul! Get out of my house! Go on! Clear off!

Scene 2: At the court.

Judge: What case do we have today?
Social worker: The lady wants a Residence Order to keep her grandson.
Judge: And what do you think?
Social worker: Well, your Honour, the mother can't even cope with her child touching her. His Nan is looking after him. So we think she should keep him.
Judge: Very well! She can have the Residence Order!

Scene 3: At the hospital.

Cherelle gives birth to Ewan and acts lovingly towards him.

Cherelle: I don't want to make the same mistakes as I did with Alex!

Cherelle gives birth to Jane, and a year or so later, to Kevin. The children frequently attend hospital with bruises, burns and sprains.

Nurse: Doctor, I'm very worried. Cherelle's not keeping her kids safe!
Doctor: We'll have to tell Social Services! The family's been here 19 times!

Scene 4: At Nan's house.

Cherelle: *(taking Ewan and Kevin)*
           Here they are! The social workers say you're to have them as they've no foster carers free to take them!

Nan:	The boys are coming to me because I'll look after them, unlike their mother! You are the worst mother a child could ever ask for!
Cherelle:	Why are you so nasty to me? What have I done to deserve it?
Nan:	Clear off! Get lost! I don't want to see you!

Scene 5: At home.

Jane returns from school to find the boys gone. Cherelle is lying on the sofa.

Jane:	Where's Ewan and Kevin?
Cherelle:	I took them to Nan's. She's looking after them.
Jane:	Now I've no one to play with! At least they won't be wrecking my room!

A few weeks later the phone rings. Cherelle hears that the boys are in foster care.

Jane:	Who is it, Mum?
Cherelle:	The social worker. She just told me the boys are in foster care. She says they're much happier! Nan kept shouting and didn't keep them clean. They've been sitting around in wet pants. I'm so relieved they're out of there! The rows have been terrible!
Jane:	Can we have tea, Mum? I'm starving! *(Cherelle lets her have milk and biscuits.)* Is this all? My tummy hurts. I'm so hungry!
Cherelle:	Pass me my pills, there's a good girl! I'd never cope without you!

A few weeks later, Cherelle is lying on the sofa. Jane tries to snuggle in close. But her mum pushes her away. Jane feels very lonely.

The therapist, in role as Cherelle, and the foster carer, as Nan, answered Jane's questions.

- -

Jane's response

Acting Scenes 1 and 2 led Jane to expressing grief at her mother having been so rejecting of her first baby, who had grown up to abuse his sister (Jane). Realising her brother's experience of rejection helped Jane to work through and make sense of painful memories of his abuse of her. Over the weeks of this play, Jane recalled her mother's descriptions of sexual abuse in her own childhood. She studied photos and mirrors to examine her resemblance to Cherelle, which alternately delighted and troubled her. The therapist explained that Cherelle had been given so little understanding or love that she had coped in the only way she knew. Cherelle had felt scared, like a child, and Jane knew her mother depended on her daughter to look after her.

From processing her experience, Jane became more expressive at acting and singing. But when her mood dipped, she would fidget, suck her thumb and roam continuously, rejecting comfort. Anxious about her prospective move, she kept worrying, 'If Mum forgets me, I'll have no right to exist'. In her permanent placement, Jane enjoyed the nurturing attention at first, but after a while, she withdrew. The intimacy of meal times proved especially testing. Stories such as those in Chapter 3 helped her to feel understood. Discovering how fictional heroes managed their predicaments encouraged Jane to find her own means of coping and rebuilt her self-esteem.

· ·

PERSONALITY DISORDER: RYAN AND LILY'S STORY

History

Ryan and Lily's birth mother, Rowena, suffered from malformation of her hips and epileptic fits and was bullied and mocked at school. Rejected by her parents, she went on to have stormy relationships and drank heavily to alleviate her pains. The children's birth father, Aidan, had moved house many times in his childhood. Feeling lonely and unwanted, he too "drowned his sorrows". After a brief attempt to "dry out", the couple became increasingly dependent on alcohol. Their problems were exacerbated by their intellectual impairment. The court's involvement led to both Rowena and Aidan being diagnosed as having personality disorders and to each of their seven children being removed from their care. Though placed for adoption in infancy, Ryan and Lily struggled to keep up at school and were often bullied. Many of their problems seemed likely to stem from pre-natal exposure to parental alcohol misuse.

The play

The play opened with Rowena being jeered at by children for her strange gait. In Scene 2 she meets her first partner and in Scene 3 we are introduced to Aidan, moving from town to town during childhood. In Scene 4, Rowena and Aidan strike up a friendship on discovering their shared experience of rejection and bullying. They stay together but Scene 5 portrays the violent outcome of their heavy drinking. A concerned neighbour contacts the police and suggests that they need help. Scene 6 has Rowena refuse to agree to her children being adopted. Understandably, some people do not want their children to grow up believing their mother agreed to give them up.

After the play

The children asked their birth mother why she had let them come into care. Rowena explains that she has never been shown any love and has had no one to show her how to be a parent or even how to cook or clean. She describes how hard it has been to cope with all her physical pains. She feels a failure, her relationship with Aidan is affected by drinking, which they do in order to seek comfort they never had from their parents. Rowena hopes that her children love their adoptive parents and feels glad that their new parents love and care for them so well.

Children's response

The children took turns to act as their birth mother. Lily appreciated how badly Rowena had suffered from mockery and rejection. When Ryan took his turn in this role, the "birth mother", on giving birth, waved away the nurse in order to drink alcohol kept hidden in the bed. They shared the parts of judge and police officer, casting the therapist and adoptive parents in supporting roles. From taking part in this play and others, Ryan and Lily discovered an aptitude for story-telling, which raised their self-esteem. Solving problems and dispensing advice in the play enabled Ryan to discover his own capabilities.

Lily had been having bad dreams in which her reflection disappeared from the mirror she was looking into. The therapist had Lily stand before a mirror to practise speaking assertively to the reflection and her nightmares faded. A painfully shy child who had hidden from visitors, Lily faced her fears and began to project her personality more confidently. Both children took up dance and drama, which improved their competence and self-confidence.

PHYSICAL ABUSE: LUCY'S STORY

History

Illness and abuse in childhood left Lucy's birth mother, Martha, depressed. The family lived in an atmosphere of violence, cruelty, squalor and infection and Lucy's father, Glen, physically abused her. Lucy recalled him locking her outside in wet weather, submerging her in icy baths and dragging her by her hair. Fearing recrimination, Martha had denied Glen's abuse. Lucy was seven when the children came into care. She was separated from her siblings and had four foster placements before she was placed for adoption. Lucy was a fearful child who had learned to repress her feelings, and needed a lot of encouragement to speak to adults. Her resentment of the foster carers' child caused intense jealousy and bitter rivalry was played out between them.

Intervention

In play therapy, Lucy recalled distressing memories of life in her birth family. She was encouraged to admit to rage at her earlier abuse and direct it at clay models of her parents. The therapist drew an outline of Lucy to help her locate the source of feelings in her body. She and the foster carer wrote down and displayed Lucy's qualities, as a collage of coloured leaves. The exercise raised Lucy's self-esteem. However, her new sense of security was to be shattered all over again when an adoptive placement was identified. Fortunately Lucy, at age 10, was placed with a very nurturing parent.

Life history play

In her adoptive home, Lucy helped to devise ten scenes for her life history play, which opened with Martha, at age 11, running away. The police bring her home but when they leave, her parents scream at her. She meets Glen, who moves in but refuses to help and constantly belittles her. Lucy is born and by Scene 4, the social worker is worried about missed appointments. Martha has two more children in quick succession. The Home Start volunteer is appalled by the mess in the family home. Martha suffers a miscarriage at home; her distress leaves Lucy frightened and powerless. The teacher expresses concern at her non-attendance at school and when officials call, the family hide. The children enter care and go through several placements. In the final scene, Lucy agrees to be adopted. Afterwards she interviewed her birth parents.

Lucy's questions to her father

Why did you lock me out in freezing weather? Why did you put me in cold baths and pull my hair? Why did Mum and I have to share the sofa while you had a double bed all to yourself? Why didn't you care about me?

Father's answers

I didn't know I was hurting you. I stopped feeling pain a long time ago. I thought you were just winding me up so I had to punish you. But you were just a little kid and what I did to you was totally out of order!

Lucy's questions to her mother

Why did you let Dad use you in the way he did? Why did you let him abuse me? Why didn't you believe me? Why did I miss going to school for weeks?

Mother's answers

I needed a man to show me an interest. Glen was the only one who did. He meant well at first. But things got worse and I was too tired and ill to stop him. It was awful seeing your bruises and scrapes! To tell the truth, I was too embarrassed to let you go to school. I'm sorry you had to go through all that. It was very wrong. But I didn't seem able to stop any of it.

I'm glad you have a nice, kind mother to look after you now. You'll have a better life than I did and I want you to make the most of it, I really do!

Lucy's response

Having had several months of therapy, Lucy was ready to accept these answers so, now focusing on her resentment of her first foster carers who had given the children inedible food, she had fun planning fictional revenge. Lucy still felt rejected by her recent carers. Her frustration at having no choice about moving made her reticent to be adopted but having her new mother acknowledge her feelings helped them bond. Lucy agreed to the adoption.

At the start of therapy, Lucy had found it hard to use her imagination, but on realising that in fiction anything can happen, especially with the help of some "magic", she grew to love story-telling and became fiercely determined to find her own solutions. A year after placement, her adoptive mother reported that Lucy, now aged 11, had made a successful transition to secondary school and her grades were steadily improving. She had made a best friend and more astonishingly, had performed on stage by herself. Lucy continues to write stories and her adoptive mother is 'incredibly proud of her'.

> The physical experience of enacting their life history enables children to make sense of the past and reconstruct their identity as survivors. By engaging parents in these plays, the "Theatre of Attachment" model can help them to make up for some of the missed experience of quality mother–infant mirroring interactions from which children discover their inner power and right to exist.
>
> Children need to trust that they will be kept safe from risk of exploitation. Drama invites sensory experience in which trauma can be reworked so that memories can be re-stored in the brain's higher cortex, thereby giving children a greater sense of control over their lives.
>
> Enacting events from the child's life, in brief snapshots and in sequential order, ensures a clarity and containment that protects them from feeling swamped. Involving parents in the play leads to enhanced, mutual understanding by creating a model for empathy, and avoiding the potential risk of children being re-traumatised. The play can be scripted or improvised. The real-life events may be portrayed, or the experience enacted in metaphor, as illustrated in the next chapter. The benefit of this style of improvisation is that children can re-write the outcome as they would like it to have been, yet acknowledge what actually happened. This helps them grieve their loss and move on to reattach, more secure in their identity as desired members of their adoptive family.

Rehearsal for living

6

If children grow up with the view that people in authority are not to be trusted, it becomes harder for them to ask for help when they need it. They may have learned that telling about something that happened to them had unforeseen consequences, for example, they were disbelieved or an allegation was denied or their family was torn apart. The child soon realises that she no longer knows whom to trust, and being dependent on her parent's love and approval, may well decide that it is safer not to divulge any further information. Other children appear to be undiscerning and will indiscriminately trust anyone.

This chapter illustrates how you can use fictional contexts to provide a safe space for children from which to address their troubling memories and worries.

Role-playing

Those who have experienced abuse and trauma often find it difficult to seek help or to admit to needing help. Giving them practice at role-playing authority figures can raise their awareness of when they need help and prepare them to use it. Roles can be practised in pairs. These pairings may include the more obvious adversaries such as police officer versus criminal, angel versus demon as well as those combinations that are commonly assumed to be complementary, such as doctor and patient, mother and child, wherein the need of one is met by the other. But the picture is not always so straightforward. After all, police officers often depend on criminal informants to help solve a crime. A social worker's job is to support the families they work with, yet their clients may perceive them as a threat, someone with the power to remove their children. The nurturing role ideally places mothers and teachers in a complementary relationship with children, but these pairings will, at times, be in conflict.

Experimenting with role pairings helps children to explore the effect of various personality types and learn how to assess trustworthiness. From the following pairings, which can be illustrated on cards, children are invited to choose a role and cast their parent in the matching one. Playing the part of someone from another generation also gives the child practice at negotiating from a different perspective.

Complementary roles

Doctor and patient	Cinderella and fairy godmother
Mother and child	Wizard and apprentice
Teacher and pupil	Driver and passenger
Social worker and client	Priest and worshipper
Salesman and customer	Waiter and diner

Adversarial roles

Police officer and criminal	Monster and angel
Judge and defendant	Witch and fairy
Warrior and pacifist	Beauty and the Beast
Magician and "tricked"	King and slave
Referee and footballer	Spider Man and Green Goblin

Examples of role play

King and slave

A child takes the role of "king", casting his mother as "slave".

King: Fetch my sword! There are enemies out there! We must fight them!
Slave: Your Majesty, will you teach me how to fight like you?
King: Yes. Now, I need my shield!
Slave: Here is your sword and shield and here is your magic ring.
King: Let us begin!

The king and slave practise fighting. The "enemy" (therapist) appears.
Several soldiers "die". But the king protects his slaves.

Slave: Thanks, your Majesty. You saved my life! I shall serve you forever! But I want to fight as skilfully as you, who can never be defeated!
King: I am the king! No one shall be allowed to threaten my land!

Judge and defendant

The child was the "judge", the therapist was the "defendant" and the mother was the "police officer".
The judge sat on a chair piled with cushions to preside over the court.

Judge: Well, tell the court what happened!
Defendant: I didn't mean to hurt him, Your Honour. This man just flew on to my car bonnet. He blocked my view, that's why I crashed into the shop!
Judge: Officer! Tell us what you think happened.
Police officer: He'd been drinking, sir! That's why he crashed!
Judge: I sentence him to three weeks in prison. And he must not drink for the next four months. Take him to the cells!
Defendant: That's not fair! I'll lose my job!
Police officer: You should have thought of that before you drank all that beer!
Judge: Take him down!

Exploring reality through fantasy

The following two examples developed from experimenting with roles of "monster" and "angel" with Dean and Sofia. Having heard their life history, the children continued to explore their feelings through play. Symbolic enactment can provide the necessary distance to enable children to gain insights without reawakening their fears, and they can enjoy the safety of play set in fantasy. Props, dressing-up clothes, masks and other items can help to physically and psychologically separate the real from the unreal.

· ·

DEAN: FEAR OF BEING EVIL

History

Dean, aged ten, had been placed for adoption with his seven-year-old sister Sofia, both of mixed heritage. They were removed seven years previously from their birth parents' drug abuse and neglect of them. Their father had been involved in a hijack. The children went through a series of placements. Dean was diagnosed with Attention Deficit Hyperactivity

Disorder and prescribed medication for two years, but he continued to struggle to meet his adoptive parents' expectations and had a picture of himself as "bad".

Dean's play

Dramatising his life history led Dean to confront his fears of being evil. In his play, he took the role of an evil monster and cast his therapist as a queen who was plagued by several monsters and begged for help. Dean changed role to become a police officer, then a Power Ranger, and finally a prince who married the queen. On the honeymoon flight to Disneyland, the monsters reappeared to terrorise them, but this time they were successfully defeated.

The monsters die!

Once upon a time, there was a Queen and a King. One day, a monster came to their palace and said, 'I'm going to kill you if you don't give me your money and jewels'. The terrified Queen passed him her bag of money and jewels but when the monster left, she called the police. The police officer said, 'I'll try to get the monster but he's very strong'. He returned with the Queen's bag, but it was empty, and explained, 'The monster was too strong and he's got two brothers!'

The next night the monster's brother, a vampire, came and asked the Queen for all her money. He said, 'I want two thousand bucks!' The Queen said, 'I can't! I haven't got it!' The vampire asked, 'What have you got then?' The frightened Queen was left with no choice but to hand over her bag again. She said, 'This is worth a lot! So don't come back!' Later, the police found her bag and brought it back again, advising her to look after it.

The next day, the third brother came to the palace. He said 'You've killed both my brothers – you will pay!' The Queen said, 'I can't pay! Anyway, I didn't kill your brothers!' The police locked all three of the monsters in jail.

That night, Frankenstein kidnapped the King (the Queen's dad), while he lay asleep, telling the Queen, 'I warned you, you'd pay!' The Queen was terribly upset. She said, 'I hope the police lock you in jail!' The police found the King and brought him home, but meanwhile he'd been forced to drink a potion that turned his face into that of a monster.

The Queen was terrified. She called the police again. They took the King back and cut his monster head off. That let his normal head grow back.

The next afternoon when the Queen came home, all three of the brother monsters were in her lounge. At first she didn't notice them. Worried about how safe the Queen was, the police told a Power Ranger to visit. The Power Ranger saw the three monsters sitting in the lounge. He stabbed them until they looked well and truly dead. The Queen was so pleased, she asked him, 'Will you marry me and be my Prince?' The Power Ranger said 'Yes!' They got married and flew to Disneyland in America for a holiday.

On the way there, the Prince opened his suitcase and saw the strongest baddie peeping out. He picked up the baddie, threw him in the air and whacked him with his sword. Then he hurled the monster to the back of the plane and stabbed him again to make sure he was dead. The Queen fetched her mobile phone to ring the police. The Prince told her, 'Don't ring them! They can't get to the plane anyway. If there are any more monsters I'll get rid of them!'

The Queen opened her bag and saw the next two strongest brothers peeping out! She screamed but the Prince threw both the baddies in the air and massacred them. They put all three heads on a stick then the Prince put his sword in the eyes of the strongest one so if he ever came back he wouldn't be able to see a thing!

Dean's response

Dean had felt abandoned by his birth parents and was very angry. Learning of his father's past involvement in a hijack made Dean afraid that he, too, was "bad". However, adopting the role of monsters and then taking on the roles of heroes to dispose of them gave him a sense of "good" inner power. Dean began to integrate the conflicting aspects of his "good" and "bad" self, his confidence enhanced on realising that he could make his own choices.

SOFIA: FEAR OF REJECTION

History

Sofia, aged seven, was born suffering from drug withdrawal and taken straight to foster care from hospital. Now placed for adoption, her new parents observed that she seemed to have no idea how to play, and could only try to copy others. But such "copying" has meaning and as Jennings (2011) advises, is an important developmental step towards learning reciprocal play. Sofia, too, feared being unable to match up to her adoptive parents' expectations of her.

Sofia's play

In her play about "Robin Hood", Sofia took the role of a fortune teller, who knew that lots of children don't have a home. She cast her therapist as Robin Hood, who gave her money to help her to find homes and to make sick people well. As they admired each other's good deeds, the fortune teller (Sofia) declared that she had heard the children (dolls) say, 'We don't like this home!' Robin Hood felt sorry for the children and proposed that a guardian angel might help. Sofia took over as guardian angel, guiding the therapist to speak for each child and express their (Sofia's own) fears of being smelly, not knowing how to cope with dirt, and being unable to sleep or stop moving. The angel gave wise advice to each child and then sang her Song of Joy, in which she expressed a desire to be beautiful, rich and admired for her kindness and generosity.

Robin Hood and the guardian angel

Once upon a time, Robin Hood met a kind fortune teller, who knew that lots of children didn't have a home. Robin Hood gave her money from the rich people to help her find a kind person to look after the children. He asked her who else needed help and would benefit from the money he collected. The fortune teller said, 'There are some old people who are very sick!' Robin Hood gave her some money to take them to the Royal Palace Hospital where the doctors made them better so they were able to return home.

As they were passing, the fortune teller heard the children say, 'We don't like this home!' Robin Hood was sad to hear about this. He asked a guardian angel to help the children.

The guardian angel spoke to each child in turn. The first child said, 'I'm so smelly! I don't know what to do!' The guardian angel advised, 'Wash every day! Then you'll smell clean!'

Another child said, 'I don't like the dirt in my room!' The guardian angel said, 'Sweep every day, or you will get bugs and things.'

A third child called Pink told the guardian angel, 'I can't stop dancing and I can't sleep!' The guardian angel advised, 'You need a good book and to listen to a song.' She told Pink that her favourite book was *Little Red Riding Hood*. Pink thanked her.

After that, the children were much happier. Together they made up a song.

Song of Joy
I am the King with the very long hair
The very long hair, the very long hair
I am the King with the very long hair
Everyone can stare!
I have a Queen, a fabulous, fabulous Queen
A fabulous Queen who's never mean, I have got a Queen!
I've got a slave called Teddy Thinner
He wants to help people eat their dinner
I help people eat their dinner, all day long!
I have a dog called Pink, and a monkey, a monkey too
Pink's got pink hair and an orange beard
And a Pink wig that fell down in the loo!
Oh woe is me and my own
Oh woe is me and my own
Oh woe is me and my own
Ho ho ho! Merry Christmas
You are a very nice King
I have a very bad skeleton
That stood too still

Sofia's response

From a starting point of displaying limited imagination and being stuck in parallel play, Sofia's skills and self-esteem increased. She produced many more plays. There was no halting her enthusiasm for rap-style poems that she wrote and sang for hours, when given the chance! Her adoptive mother, in reflecting on the changes that she saw in Sofia in response to this therapeutic play, described her adoptive daughter as like 'a flower opening up to the sun'.

Exploring personality types in everyday settings

Using everyday settings such as a school, park, shop or doctor's surgery, children can be invited to explore the impact of various personalities and attitudes. With this aim, a play set in a shop began with an adoptive child, Tia, aged six, taking the role of cashier. Her adoptive father and therapist joined in the play.

Shame!

Once upon a time at the supermarket, a customer (therapist) arrived with a distressed baby and demanded help to stop him crying. The cashier (Tia) advised her, 'Go to the baby section and buy him something!' At the baby section, the baby pointed to a pink case. The mum said, 'He wants that one but I can't afford it!' Feeling sorry for her, the cashier gave her some money. But the baby cried for a matching scarf and gloves. Mum said, 'I've had enough!'

She dumped the baby on a kind man (adoptive father) saying, 'You look after him!' He said, 'But your baby needs you!' She replied, 'I don't care! I've had enough!' The police officer (Tia) took the mother to prison. She cried, 'It's not fair! I didn't mean it!' The police officer replied, 'You should have thought of that when you had a baby to look after!'

On release, the mother returned to the shop. The cashier (Tia) said, 'Hands up anyone who has been in prison!' Told to raise her hand, the mum said, 'It's my mother's fault! She never showed me how to be a mum!' Unimpressed, the cashier replied, 'You are a grown-up so you should act like one and not blame someone else when you get everything wrong!' Mum wailed, 'I just want my baby back!' But she took things and didn't pay so returned to prison. On release, she went back to the shop and moaned about her mum. The cashier said, 'Pretend you are little and have a second chance'. Grandma (therapist) said, 'I want to look after you properly this time!' But baby's Mum didn't learn anything and was sent to a very cold place. She moaned about the cold, so was sent to a hot place and died of heat stroke. But her baby was well cared for and loved his new parents.

How the story helped

Through this play, Tia was trying to make sense of generational patterns of inadequacy. From observing that Grandma had not taken care of the baby's mother, she showed her determination to make adults take responsibility for their crimes – Tia sent the mother to places of intolerable cold and heat until she died. In so doing, Tia was exacting revenge for her abandonment. The play enabled Tia to reconcile to life in her nurturing adoptive family. Tia then began to rehearse predicaments that she found challenging.

Learning to be co-operative

Neglected children typically struggle to recognise the unwritten social rules that sustain relationships as they find it hard to know how to "be" with new people. The following play was directed by Tia but gave the adults involved an opportunity to demonstrate how confusing life can be for an individual who has not been taught the social rules. Tia cast her adoptive mother as the angel, while the therapist acted as the pirate, being exaggeratedly bossy, careless and oblivious to social cues. The fairy (Tia) tried various strategies to gain the pirate's co-operation. But the pirate, to avoid being reprimanded, refused to own up to having bumped into the angel, which then placed the fairy in a difficult position, often faced by parents who don't know which account to believe. The pirate persisted in asking for advice on how to change and to be shown how to behave.

How to be nice

Once upon a time, an angel was looking after a fairy. Seeing a pirate approach, she called, 'Where is my beautiful fairy?' The pirate reached the fairy first and told her, 'I'm going to take your wand!' The fairy made a spell, saying, 'I'm turning you into a frog!' Landing in a chilly pond, the frog croaked, 'I hate the cold!' The fairy said, 'You should have thought of that before you tried to take my wand!' The fairy asked kindly, 'Will you be nice if I let you be a pirate again?' The pirate said, 'I'll try!' The fairy reversed the spell and turned him back into a pirate. He asked, 'What must I do to make you like me? What are the rules?' She told him to cook the dinner, help with cleaning and be nice.

The pirate couldn't cook so the angel showed him how to make chicken nuggets and chips. Then she had to show him how to vacuum. The pirate complained that he didn't like all this work and wasn't used to it! The angel commented, 'He's always moaning!' The fairy replied, 'I told him to be nice!' The pirate said, 'Yes, but how?' The fairy advised, 'Try walking nicely!' But the pirate kept bumping into the angel, insisting 'It wasn't me!'

Well, the fairy didn't know who to believe! Eventually, she and the angel had him walking straight. They took him to the ice rink where the fairy patiently showed him how to skate. The pirate learned how to be nice, thanks to the fairy's good example. She twirled her wand again and turned the pirate into another fairy. And they lived happily ever after, at least whenever they weren't having an argument!

••

How the play helped

Tia gained confidence firstly from discovering that she actually knew most of the social rules and manners required of children; secondly, from her adoptive parents' emotional availability in being receptive and sensitive. She made progress in sustaining friends and playing more co-operatively with her sister.

Learning problems

When a three-year-old sucks his thumb, disrupts children's games, throws tantrums, or vehemently denies taking someone's chocolate despite the evidence, we are not surprised. We forgive actions that we attribute to his age and understanding. But when this behaviour is displayed by a much older child of, say, 10 to 13 years of age, it appears out of place because we expect children to act according to their chronological age. If children are bigger than average size, expectations are raised, which can encourage the secure, capable child to meet or exceed them. However, children who display unusually immature behaviour due to intellectual, social and emotional delay are more likely to elicit disapproval, bullying and condemnation. Negative attitudes affect their self-esteem and can make them inclined to "give up".

One sign of low self-esteem and deep unhappiness is not caring about personal hygiene. Children who have been neglected and untrained during their early years can find it difficult to remember what is expected of them in their new families, which will have rules and routines they may not have grown up with.

•••

PEARL: HYGIENE ISSUES

Pearl, aged nine, and adopted when she was four, was not intellectually delayed, but because she had missed the "mirroring" of healthy mother–infant interactions, she failed to recognise many of the social cues that most of us take for granted. Pearl had also become resistant to the routines of having a shower and cleaning her teeth and more recently had ceased to change her underwear. Her adoptive parents perceived this behaviour as a control issue, but Pearl's resistance almost certainly stemmed from early neglect and her fear of water. During her first three years in her birth family, she had suffered the trauma of being repeatedly scalded and plunged into cold baths.

From a selection of finger puppets, Pearl chose a magician and two pirates. She gave her therapist the magician while she and Mum took the pirates. The play opened with Pearl's pirate asking the magician (therapist) to conjure up a pet tiger. The magician obliged and (the therapist taking advantage of the privacy of this being a fantasy) complained about how smelly the pirates were. But the pirates maintained that they didn't want to wash. The magician shared his worry that, if they didn't wash, the pirates soon wouldn't have any friends left. He asked them why they didn't wash. Pearl's pirate now admitted that he could not really remember what to do, while Mum's pirate declared that he didn't care for washing anyway, or for having his hair brushed.

Now that the root of the problem had been identified, the magician's desire to help prompted Pearl's pirate to ask if he could "magic" them to want to wash. So the magician cast spells with rhyming chants: *Izzy Wizzy, Let's get busy wizzy washing*, and *Abracadabra allacazzoo, I'm going to make a washer of you!* Now "enchanted", the pirates agreed that the magician's spells worked!

The Smellies

Once upon a time, there were two pirates called Stinky and Smelly who never washed or brushed their hair and teeth. Well, these pirates wanted some unusual pets so they asked the magician if he would conjure up a tiger, which he promptly did. Then they wanted a baboon so the magician made a spell and conjured up a baboon.

By now, the magician had noticed an unpleasant smell and hoped it would go away soon. Well, it didn't, so he told the pirates that he didn't like the smell. But they didn't mind it so the magician said people might like them more if they smelled better. The pirates said they had forgotten how to wash. They asked the magician if he could magic them not to be smelly. The magician made a spell that worked. Suddenly the pirates were clean! 'But can you stay clean?' asked the magician. They weren't sure. He gave them a parrot that squawked: 'Have a wash! Clean your teeth! Brush your hair!' The parrot made them laugh and helped them remember what to do at the required times, every day, so from then on the pirates washed happily!

What helped

Pearl drew posters of the parrot and wrote the advice in speech bubbles. She put them up in her bedroom and the hygiene problem was resolved.

But Pearl remained dependent on her adoptive mother for guidance in what to do and say in social situations. To gain the practice she needed, she was encouraged to play scenes such as "Going to the Doctors" and "Coffee mornings". Accordingly, one "mother" (pretended to) phone her friend. Then she (Mum) knocked at the door of her friend's (Pearl's) house, but, despite her announcing 'I'm knocking at the door', Pearl failed to respond accurately, and picked up the phone instead. Yet, after many patient attempts she learned how to respond to particular cues. Further scenes, set in a fictitious supermarket, which involved plenty of role changes, helped Pearl to recognise more of these social cues.

Reflecting on the play

After play, we need to make time to reflect on the feelings that have been aroused in the process. In drama, a lot can happen in a short time and the child's sequences can become confusing for adults to follow. For this reason, it is useful to invite the child to recall the action that actually took place from their perspective, which often differs from that of parents. You could ask the child if there were any surprises, whether the characters responded as expected, or as the child wanted them to. You could discuss what the main characters need from each other at the conclusion of the story. You could ask what advice one character would give another. For instance, in the story above, the magician could say how he would like things to turn out for the pirates and ask what would help or what might get in the way? An older and verbally competent child could be invited to decide on the "moral" of the story and to think about what each character learned from their adventures. To chart the progress that results from children's engagement in this kind of imaginative play, see Chapter 7.

Children love to see their stories and plays printed, especially with pictures that illustrate them and help enhance meaning. Re-reading the stories together reinforces learning and helps them to realise how many skills they have developed and how many answers they have found to particular dilemmas, albeit fictionally. All these skills are transferable to daily life and children's imagination will expand when they are encouraged to experiment.

Giving children practice at playing adversarial and complementary roles enables them to recognise when help is necessary and of value, and also to acknowledge the effects of the misuse of power. When children are uncertain as to whom they can trust, play gives them an opportunity to make sense of their confusion and build new relationships. Props and costumes serve to specify the boundaries of play and help children to distinguish fantasy from reality. Meanwhile, the privacy of fantasy offers the distance that allows children to feel safe and gain power over dealing with their oppressive experiences.

Everyday settings can be used in fictional contexts to explore the effects of various attitudes and behaviours. Children can use these scenarios to make sense of the bewildering behaviour and attitudes of caregivers who have let them down in the past. From comparing these negative past experiences with the different way they are treated now, they discover that some adults can be trusted. In the course of finding out which strategies are effective, they learn the unwritten social rules.

Moreover, children with low self-esteem can be helped to confront personal problems and find new ways to manage them in the privacy of these scenarios. Their self-esteem is raised when they realise how much they have learned and see their stories recorded/printed and illustrated. Inevitably, feelings will be stirred when parents and children participate in such activities together, and this sharing of emotional experience brings children and parents emotionally closer, which helps children feel safer to attach.

7

Charting children's progress

Helping children to come to terms with their history is argued to be the most effective way to prevent patterns of re-victimisation. Until they are able to understand what happened to them, traumatised children struggle to use words to describe their feelings. Our task, as the adults involved in meeting their needs, is to name their feelings and, as Geddes (2006) advises, help them move from unbearable feelings to 'thinkable thoughts'.

The first part of this chapter explores the progress that children make in play in which they address their earlier experiences. The second part proposes markers for evaluating their progress and discusses the impact of this work on both parents and children involved in the play.

The stories that children tell

We begin with the stories children create as their way of making sense of their life and relationships. The methods illustrated focus on the needs of traumatised children whose "fight-flight-freeze" responses can feel threatening both to themselves and to the adults attempting to care for them. The child can feel "cut off" until he is understood and can "lay his ghosts to rest". Le Vay (2011) quotes Pennebaker and Seagal's (1999) finding that:

…the more coherent and organised an account an individual creates in relation to past trauma the greater the likelihood of beneficial claims. (Le Vay, 2011, p.187)

The impact of empathy

Empathy is often described as the capacity or drive to "step into another's shoes" and "see through their eyes". Baron-Cohen and Chakrabarti (2008) clarify that empathy involves not merely recognising the feelings of another but having the ability to feel the other person's feeling in your own self and to give an appropriate emotional response. It is generally held that we have to experience empathy in order to be capable of giving it. This begins with the mirroring interactions from which, optimally, infants gain a sense of self and their right to be in the world. Neglected children tend to miss out on this experience. Patterns of abuse and trauma can also continue through generations. However, a longitudinal (30-year) study of interfamilial transfer of traumatising experience (Sroufe *et al*, 2005) found that if a child in safer care is in an empathic relationship for at least six months, the negative pattern may not be perpetuated. To be sincere and careful of children's feelings is to model caring attitudes.

When children feel overwhelmed, it is especially helpful to acknowledge their feelings, saying, for example: 'How painful and frightening this must feel' or 'How very harsh!' In play, an adult can interview the key character: 'Hello Tiger! What's it like in your jungle? Are you having fun? (or) Is it scary? Do you need anything? What would you like to happen?' The child might tell you about Tiger's feelings, which are likely to represent his own. A troubled child who is verbally articulate may share more of her thoughts if the adult shows deep interest, perhaps saying, 'Help me to understand this'. The following vignettes, which illustrate children's progress through storymaking, demonstrate the effective use of empathy, and begin with Surinder's story.

SURINDER'S STORY OF LOSS AND IMPRISONMENT

History

Surinder, aged six, was born in India. Two years earlier her mother had died and relatives brought her to the UK to live with them. These relatives were deeply unhappy and soon resented the demands of another child on their ever-dwindling resources. They abused their own children and demanded that Surinder be taken into local authority care. She settled well with white foster carers but her relatives felt unhappy about her being with people of a different ethnicity so took her back and searched for adopters from their own community. Social workers became worried that Surinder would be taken by people who had not been approved, and on learning that she had been illegally moved to a couple, who possibly wanted to adopt her, they removed her and placed her in foster care again. An acrimonious situation developed, which left Surinder feeling treated like a piece of property and yearning to be valued for who she was.

Intervention

Still grieving for the loss of her mother, Surinder had painted pictures of her life in India. Living with her mentally sick relatives in the UK had felt like being locked up. In a sand tray, Surinder developed a story featuring dangerous creatures misusing their magic by sending the "good" creatures to a different country, where they landed in jail. Her fears were projected in the form of a monster. The therapist reflected, 'How terrifying, being locked up – no one to rescue them!' and asked, 'What's it like in there?' Surinder drew the princess in jail, looking scared. Validation of her fears led her to effect a rescue.

The great escape

Once upon a time, a long time ago, there was a pony and a helping tiger, a turtle, a magic dragon called Puff, a panda, a big cheetah, a lion, a ballerina and Princess Layla.

One day some witches with pink spooky hair came to the Spooky Hair Forest. The lion said 'ROAR!' Then a crocodile said, 'Hello! My name is Crocodile! I snap all the time! Snap, Snap, Snap! That's what crocodiles do!'

Puff the magic dragon made all the animals disappear to the cheapest place in a different country. The friends cried, 'Something is wrong! We need to get out of here!' They pulled a big handle in the ground and landed in jail with some kind animals, Tiger, Cheetah and Panda.

No one came to rescue them. A big monster told them, 'You will have to stay here forever!' They were very scared. Princess Layla asked, 'How shall we escape?' But none of them knew. Luckily, Tiger was very strong and pulled at the window bars until they bent under his weight. Tiger escaped through the window and waited for the others to follow. The others climbed out on Cheetah's back. Now free, they looked for a safe home!

How the story helped

Creating this story of imprisonment enabled Surinder to recognise the courage and persistence that she needed to keep explaining to decision makers why she did not wish to live with the adopters whom she could not trust. Eventually, having convinced them that the match was not viable, she was adopted by her foster carer, who loved her for the person that she was. As Surinder's trust and confidence grew, her learning accelerated.

MARK'S STORY OF CONFUSION

History

Mark, aged nine, had been adopted at four years of age from foster care and now lived with his adoptive father, who had separated from Mark's adoptive mother. She and their 15-year-old son now lived with her same-sex partner. Mark's resistance to visiting his adoptive mother and brother was driving a wedge between his parents, who felt they were being "played off" against each other. Their conflicts mirrored the acrimony between Mark's alcohol-dependent birth parents. At school, his distracting behaviour had been alienating his peers and teachers.

Intervention

Using toys in the sand tray, Mark explored the dichotomy of "good" versus "bad", a characteristic of younger children, who, in the egotistical stage of "magical thinking" (Fraiberg, 2008), assume that their wishes, good or bad, will be realised. The protagonists in his story searched for a new home where they would "fit in". The army and the Simpson family represent opposing factions and the conflict over territory echoed Mark's recollection of domestic warfare. Repeated threats, bombs, snakes in disguise and the presence of someone dressed as a doctor with apparent intent to deceive, indicated Mark's fear and confusion about whom he could trust. Externalising his worries and fears through the character of Bob empowered Mark to dispose of the threatening elements in his story and to resolve matters by creating an outcome that satisfied him.

Defence of the army base

Once upon a time, there were some soldiers living on an army base. One day, the Simpsons decided to visit. They said, 'Hey! Can we come in?' The army people said 'No!' They all started fighting because the Simpsons really wanted to go in but the army didn't want them! The Simpsons tried to get to the camp by helicopter – they didn't know it was broken! They tried hard but found the base was centrally locked.

Some homeless trolls asked the soldiers if they could live in the camp. The soldiers agreed because the trolls were so cute. They let a zebra in as well. Now they needed more space to fit everyone in. But Bob the Builder came by, shouting to them, 'You can't put houses here!' The soldiers replied, 'We've already built on this land!' Bob said, 'I'm going to knock it down!' He was in such a nasty mood!

Next, a load of snakes came along and bit people. A soldier from another team tried to blow up the base but the radar stopped him! The grenade car set off a bomb, shocking the soldier. People ran away, scared. Someone dressed as a doctor came rushing along, smashing everything down. He was on the other side, in disguise! The fences were blown up! Snakes wriggled away. A man shot the plane and all the cars drove off. Trolleys sank. The battle lasted all night. But they got the zebras back as camouflage and the soldiers shot all the baddies. Now that the army base was safe, they all lived happily ever after.

How the story helped

As his adoptive parents realised the extent of Mark's confusion, they began to communicate more regularly, which stabilised his relationship with each of them and resolved the contact problem. At school, Mark's concentration improved and his grades rose steadily. Practice at resolving disputes in fictional play situations helped Mark to make and sustain his friendships.

JOSIE'S STORY OF ABUSE

History

Josie, aged six, recently placed with her younger sister for adoption, was one of four children removed from a family steeped in sexual abuse. Reports described the birth parents as weak and controlled by the extended family with whom they lived. Josie was emotionally stuck and struggling to adapt.

Intervention

Josie's collage of a "deep sea" scene developed into her rescue story. She viewed parent figures as unreliable. The king and queen, although featuring in her picture, did not enter her story, in which trapped princesses demand to be rescued. Noticing lots of smoke, the therapist observed that the princesses might be scared and confused by the smoke that was making them choke and obscuring their view. Josie did not think the princesses would be rescued. The efforts of various princes prove unsuccessful, perhaps because in Josie's experience, the conventional sources of help (the police) had proved largely ineffectual.

Curiously, the source of rescue was a fish (the slipperiness and smell of which may subconsciously be reminiscent of sexual abuse). At first, it covers the house (implying secrecy) wherein lives a girl that no one likes. The therapist commented on how upsetting it must be for the girl to be disliked. In response, Josie said the girl turned out to also be a princess and found a nice new house. Josie made clay "rock people" who she said were from the North Pole (like her first home, reported to be cold and bare) and gave them her own and her sister's names. Josie was thrilled with her (clay) models.

To the rescue

Once upon a time, there were three princesses called Cinderella, Snow Queen and Snow White. They lived together in a castle but they were trapped. Lots of smoke was coming out. Snow Queen and Snow White told Cinderella to get help. 'Help!' cried Cinderella, who then told her sisters 'Hey! I shouldn't have to be calling for help, *you* should!'

Prince Charming came along and tried to get Cinderella out, like princes always did when a heroine was stuck! Anyway, they were still stuck. Prince Percy came and tried to rescue Snow White but couldn't so he shouted 'Help!' The last prince came along and got trapped too.

There was a girl living in a house who no one liked. The fish came and covered the house. They all called 'Help!' again but at first the fish didn't hear. They called harder and went round all the houses. In the end the fish heard them and jumped. The princesses and little girl found a nice house and lived happily ever after.

How the story helped

Through her experiments in play, Josie realised the kind of attitudes that she liked and disliked, a discovery that heightened her self-awareness. She responded to the privacy afforded by fantasy play, and would almost certainly have shrunk from more direct comparisons being made with her real life.

Josie found it difficult to cope in certain situations, especially going to school, shopping, and to places of entertainment. She created plays set in these contexts and practised ways to "be" with people. This helped to build her confidence and to enable her to progress, and she began to settle and sustain friendships.

JOEL: PROBLEMS WITH SELF-CONTROL

History

Joel, aged six, was in his second adoptive placement, this time with his younger brother. Joel had been abused and neglected, and had endured many moves. He was jealous of his younger brother, who had been removed at birth and had attached securely to their new parents. Feeling alienated, Joel expected to be rejected and moved on again. His lengthy tantrums made life for his new parents feel like a constant battle. They asked for life history work to help Joel to understand why he had had to keep moving, as they wanted to reassure him that he was staying with them.

Intervention

Joel loved playing with "hero toys" to develop his stories. In *Brains are best*, the main character admits: 'I'm tired but I want my boss to be proud of me', thus revealing Joel's desire to impress his adoptive father. But threats, symbolising Joel's fears, loom constantly, in the form of invasions by enemies. Reflecting on how exhausting life must be for these brave Power Rangers, the therapist asks if anyone could help. 'Perhaps they could go to hospital?' Joel has the injured Power Rangers made better. In so doing, he acknowledges that help can be beneficial. Strong guys enter the narrative to protect the friends from further trouble. Josh's surprise at his boss knowing where he lives reflects Joel's anxiety as to who can be trusted. He perceives the slightest criticism as proof of his being unworthy. Yet, when baddies turn nasty, Josh and his Power Ranger friends plan and succeed in outwitting them. Joel reached his own conclusion that, for solving problems, brains are best!

Brains are best!

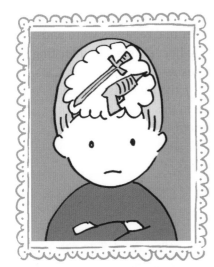

One day, Josh went to the office and three Power Rangers called Tommy, Ben and Jack came along, asking if he would like some help. Josh replied, 'Yes please! You can do all the work. I'm tired but I want my boss to be proud of me!'

Tommy asked, 'What do you want us to do?' Josh said, 'Sort out those wrestlers!' A naughty goblin started fighting with the three Power Rangers. Josh didn't see, as he was asleep in another part of the building. It's just as well there were three of them as Ben and Jack were so badly injured they had to go to hospital. Jack told the nurse what had happened. Back at the office, Tommy asked some strong guys to come round and stop the nasty goblin from causing any more trouble!

Josh went home and got changed. His manager came to Josh's house and asked, 'What's all that mess?' Josh said, 'There isn't a mess! Anyway, how do you know where my house is?' The manager said, 'Easy! I followed you!'

Josh went to his wrestling club, put on his mask and gloves and won the first fight. A tough guy challenged the Power Rangers and the goblin to a fight. The Power Rangers put their helmets on. They threw the baddies out of the ring. Josh and the Power Rangers won. When Silver Ranger arrived, there was one more fight. The worst thing was that Silver Ranger turned against Josh's friends. The fight turned a bit nasty. But Josh's friends used their brains and weapons to trick the baddies, which just showed that "Brains are best!"

How the story helped

In the course of enacting this tale of repeated betrayals, including by the heroes' friend, Silver Ranger, having his feelings acknowledged helped Joel to realise that making plans was more efficient than fighting without armour. Now that he felt wanted, Joel was more able to control his strong feelings. Impressed, his teacher asked him to mentor another pupil in his class.

ZARA'S STRUGGLE FOR IDENTITY

History

Zara, aged 10, had rarely met her Asian father. She had been brought up by her white British mother and was now in foster care. While exploring her life history, Zara initially recalled pleasurable memories of birthday parties and presents, and then of hunger that had forced her to eat leaves from the hedge. She expressed her disgust at her mother going to drug parties and leaving her with a neighbour. Zara often dreamt of her mother smiling at her yet being out of her reach. She was afraid that her mother, who had failed to attend contact visits, would die and that the police might not know of Zara's whereabouts to inform her of her mother's death.

Intervention

On hearing a story in which cats from rival families have a litter of kittens, Zara identified with the kitten that looked "different". Making and painting clay cats led to her telling the story *Petal's adventures*, in which she explored her confusion about who her real relatives were and who the new arrivals in her foster home were, who instantly became her "sisters". In adjusting to a new culture, it seemed to Zara that one had to make up the rules as one went along. Cats are generally expected to take food that is left out, yet in Zara's story, the therapist noticed that they were punished for eating the leftovers. Zara admitted that in this foster home she expected harsh remonstrations if she helped herself to snacks without asking.

Petal's adventures

Once upon a time, there was a cat called Petal. The cat lived in a palace but didn't realise that another cat lived there until one day she met Elvis in one of the bedrooms. Then another cat came to the palace. Petal found out that it was her sister! Lots of humans lived in this palace too.

One day they had a party. The hungry cats smelled the food so they went to the kitchen and ate the party food while the people were watching a movie. When the people found out, they were very cross and shut the cats outside.

But it was pouring with rain! What a punishment for being hungry!

How the story helped

Zara admitted that she often felt "different", confused about her identity and, particularly, to whom she owed any loyalty. Craving nurture, she had begun to imitate the younger children in her placement in ways that annoyed her carer. Including the carer in play helped her to understand Zara while allowing her to work through early developmental stages.

Zara loved dressing up as a baby animal and directed the adults to take the roles of parent, guard or trainer. As a lion cub, she asked to be 'fed, entertained and put to bed'. Her owner (therapist) then trained the cub to guard the palace in case they were burgled. This required Zara to think about others' expectations and to make a plan. Accordingly, the lion cub frightened off a burglar who was then jailed. Zara began to mature and she made a successful transition to her permanent placement.

CALLUM'S STORY OF FEELING CRUSHED

History

Callum, aged six, and his four-year-old sister were in foster care as a result of their mother's drug abuse and violent relationships. She had favoured her daughter but frequently left Callum in charge. On more than one occasion, she had fallen into a drug-induced coma, and left the chip pan to catch fire. Six-year-old Callum had called the rescue services. Although he and his sister had a kinship bond of sorts, they were highly intolerant of each other, which made the task of parenting them together immensely stressful.

Intervention

Callum's story about an avalanche evolved from clay modelling. The land splitting was evocative of his world having split apart when he was taken from his mother. She remained in a small dark flat in town, while Callum and his sister were living in a large house in the country. The power of water causing 'houses to be swept out to sea' may, for Callum, have represented the adults' power to make decisions on his behalf, over which he had no influence. The avalanches that came one after another symbolised his feeling of being overwhelmed. Like those who must "keep swimming" if they are not to drown, he tries to keep going. Callum wanted to believe in a God with the power to rebuild the world, but saw his situation as a battle against even greater forces. Yet the therapist reflecting: 'How terrifying – so much disaster!' and allowing him to play out many more catastrophic scenes helped him cope with a seemingly indefinite and exhausting wait for a decision about his future.

The avalanche

The land split. Water rushed through. As the sides caved in, people fell into the water. A dam was built to stop the flood but the water was more powerful and the force of it knocked the bridge down. There was an avalanche. Earth and stones crashed down and covered the trees and land. Again, the people made a bridge from the trees to the other side of the river but the water got past easily. It went under the bridge, rose up and knocked the bridge down. God threw the earth out of the sea. There had been three houses along one side of the river but now there were only two. The water swept up the earth and sent both the houses out to sea. The people had to keep swimming around in the sea or drown. God started making big mountains, trees and rocks but an avalanche came and made the land as flat as a desert. God built more trees and mountains, but yet another avalanche crushed them. It was icy. They dug deep to see if any people were still alive!

How the story helped

In seeking a resolution that would satisfy him, Callum realised that his growing belief in God was enabling him to contemplate the possibility of a greater force of good to counter evil. After two years in foster care, he was placed for adoption. Although Callum was relieved to be separated from his sister in his new family, he began to feel restricted by rules he was unused to. His adoptive parents' necessary vigilance seemed oppressive to him. However, they made time to play with him every day and, after a few weeks, he felt more secure. Yet at school Callum continued to struggle to manage relationships; the other children found him bossy and controlling. Survival stories encouraged him to practise ways of coping with the situations that caused him difficulties.

··

LISA: DISTORTED RELATIONSHIPS

History

Lisa, aged seven, and her sister, aged five, were in foster care awaiting decisions about their future. They had witnessed violence between their mother and her latest partner and it was alleged that Lisa had been sexually abused by her mother's partners. Unsurprisingly, Lisa was jealous of her little sister who was favoured by their mother and their foster carer.

Intervention

In Lisa's story, fairies (like Lisa) experience their mother as selfish, ruthless and disregarding of conventional social rules. The protagonist is nameless, as if not entitled to an identity of her own, in common with children who sublimate their needs in order to assuage those of their parents, so as to avoid disapproval.

In the story, the fairy discovers that she has a sister but (since Lisa anticipates rejection) her attempt to make friends is rebuffed. Similarly to children who reveal their true feelings when grown-ups are not looking, the dog bites the second fairy to punish her for rejecting her sister's overtures. When the swing breaks, the queen knows she must pay. (Lisa used to have to remind her mother to change nappies and make meals.) Becoming a fairy could have made the prince a companion for the protagonist but the queen steals a wand to turn him into her own suitor.

The therapist commented, 'How selfish the queen is! The fairy is so brave and strong!' Recognising that she bore aspects of the fairy's personality and talents encouraged Lisa to keep going.

The selfish queen

Algernon the dog, a Fairy and her mother, the Queen, went in search of playmates. They found one called Alice who said, 'Don't you know I'm your sister?' The Fairy replied, 'No I didn't! I want to play with you!' But Alice said 'No!' The Queen told them, 'You must always share things!' But she wasn't looking when Algernon ran and bit Alice for saying 'No'.

They went to the park and the dog broke their favourite swing. The Queen had to pay £100 for a new one and 2p for each fairy to play on it. After that they went to a castle and magicked a Prince into a fairy. The fairy liked him but because he was so handsome, the Queen stole her wand and turned him into a man she could marry. The Queen wanted to kiss him but they fell out, which was a shame since now they were married they were no longer allowed to kiss each other.

The Prince and Queen separated and built their own houses. She helped him build his house next door in case they wanted to fall in love again. They went back to the castle to look for treasure to ensure they would live happily ever after. But a King came and asked the Prince, 'Why are you here?' He turned to the Queen and said, 'Have you forgotten you were married to me?' The Queen told the Prince, 'Sorry, he's my husband too. Now I've got two. I can't decide which one to live with!' She chose the King because he was richer. After all, she was the Queen and is entitled because it's "ladies before gentlemen"!

• •

How the story helped

Exploring her confusion over her mother's relationships and betrayals helped Lisa to accept the nurture given in her foster placement. When she and her sister were placed for adoption, Lisa continued to fear rejection, but after two years, she came to trust and attach more securely to her adoptive parents.

Charting progress

By playing with their children, adoptive parents and foster carers can replicate the early experience of quality mother–infant interactions that neglected children have missed. Through continual practice at play, even children who are developmentally delayed learn to engage in "make believe". Relaxation, enjoyment and laughter help to build the trust necessary for children to be able to work through the complexities of their feelings and experiences. Research (Russ, 2004; Russ and Niec, 2011) shows that children who develop imagination and problem-solving skills in play cope better with stress and are able to think of more ways to react when they are faced by stress-inducing situations that require control of aggression. Play also enhances children's skills in making and maintaining relationships, and by practising the expression of a range of emotions, children verbalise more fluently. Parents can help by commenting on their actions and the feelings expressed. Their empathy will help children become open to their suggestions as to possible outcomes (see Chapter 1).

Why evaluate?

Evaluation can bring feelings of dread for those of us who regard it as a chore or "another gun to shoot us with". Results of interventions that aim to change feelings and behaviour can be intangible and subjective as it is always hard to know the precise links between activity and outcome or how a particular activity leads to a particular result. Yet, if we do not measure progress, how do we know that our efforts have been worthwhile? Noticing changes can encourage persistence in the pursuit of goals. Hogarth and Comfort (2010, p.17) observe that evaluation 'can motivate and help people see how far they have come, and what they have learned and to decide their next steps'. It can also help to bring closure, enabling us to say "goodbye" and "thank you".

Children who have traumatic pasts generally continue to be troubled by unexpected triggers. Memories of trauma being held in the emotional part of the brain (dictating "fight-flight-freeze" responses) can make progress slow and hard to achieve. Identifying the source of trauma can help the child to adjust their responses by noticing the physiological sensations that cause their body to react in the way that it does.

Preceding chapters have described how setting a creative flow in motion brings to consciousness those memories and fears that children have previously been unable to articulate. In my "Theatre of Attachment" model, I have found that organising fragmented experience into meaningful narratives and repeating these narratives in various ways, so as to "explain without blame", desensitises children from the pain of their traumatising memories. Since the main task is to enable the children to make sense of what has happened to them, the process of "co-constructing" the meaning of these experiences (White, 2007) becomes more important than the end product. But how do we identify whether or not our intervention is helping children to progress?

Evaluation tools

Various tools are used to assess the effectiveness of play and related therapeutic interventions that address emotional and behavioural difficulties. Established tools used pre- and post-intervention to measure change in children include the Goodman Strengths and Difficulties Questionnaire (SDQ) and, more recently grown to prominence, the Boxall Profile, developed for nurture groups in schools. A difficulty concerning these tools is that they focus attention on the child who becomes identified as the "problem". But children's attachments and their interactions are affected both by their experience and by the attitudes of their parents and carers towards them. Attachment develops in the context of a dyadic relationship, so children react differently to different carers with different attachment styles (Crittenden, 2009).

Nevertheless, to pinpoint the need for, or success of, an intervention, it is necessary to understand the issues that provoked the request for help in the first place, so that they can be compared with how the child presents before, during and after the intervention. Therefore, it is useful for adoptive parents and foster carers who require specialised support to list their worries about and perceptions of the child and to examine how their own reactions might be influenced by the past. This will help to evaluate change as a result of intervention. The markers for evaluating progress proposed here are based on practice wisdom. They overlap with the established tools but include additional markers developed by myself, which relate to children's capacity for creativity. First, let us define the range and extent of the problems.

The adoptive parents/foster carers

- History of childhood: loss, bullying, trauma and age at the time
- Health problems affecting energy and emotional capacity
- Problematic relationships, past and current
- Experience of being parented
- Expectations of child, as affected by own experience and ambitions
- Availability and attitudes of family and friends
- Issues related to culture, heritage, religion, disability

The children

Developmental history

- Early history, including pre- and post-natal experience of drugs, alcohol, violence, separations and moves
- Inherited genes; propensity for mental or developmental problems

Current situation

- What frightens the child, e.g. water, journeys, frowns, bedtime, illness?
- Health issues: sleep disturbance, enuresis, eating, bowel control
- School performance, capacity to make and sustain friends
- Ability to play and use creative materials
- Relationships at home
- Child's understanding and acceptance of the past
- Is the child too fearful or too trusting?

Measuring emotional impact during the course of play

- Observe the child's eyes for signs of emotion such as excitement, irritability, relief, anger; loss of control of their limbs such as shaking; speed of movement and gait. The child's reaction to particular situations will help identify their expression of unresolved feelings.
- How does the child make you feel? Included but pushed around or excluded and ignored? This will help to identify attachment patterns.
- Notice the frequency and variety of the child's emotional expression: does he name feelings expressed by characters in the play? Is there secrecy? Does she take risks or avoid them?
- Observe how the child organises their play: how long do they spend "sorting" rather than developing action or dialogue? What does this indicate about their age and stage of functioning?
- Note the quality and complexity of the story as indicators of the capacity for more advanced creativity and problem-solving skills.
- What themes or dichotomies are prevalent in the play?
- How much does the child use their imagination? What aspects of their story are unique, or "copied" from stories they already know?
- Does the child elaborate or embellish stories or a familiar tale?
- What evidence is there of nurturance in the child's play or story?
- How flexible or receptive is the main character to ideas or solutions or offers of help? Are reciprocity and emotional (shared) understanding present?
- Is the action in the story appropriate, contingent with the setting?
- Does the child treat materials with respect?
- Does the child enjoy being creative? Does she show aspects of divergent thinking, or rely mainly on predictive outcomes?

Next, let us consider the pattern of overall progress to determine effectiveness of play for the child. These measurements consider the whole child, including imagination and relational skills, control of affect (the expression of feeling), health and self-care, progress in school and in relationships at home.

Observing progress at conclusion of intervention

Development of imagination and relational skills

1 Does the child have the ability to take a fictional role and tell a story that shows a sequence of events? Is there a beginning, middle and end?

2 Does the child find solutions to previously irresolvable dilemmas? Has she become less dependent on reassurance, or require more?

3 Is the child willing to explore a wider range of play opportunities?

4 Has the child learned to use materials age-appropriately? (Inappropriate use might consist of excessive waste and "flitting" between activities.)

5 Does the child connect characters' feelings to his own feelings?

6 Can the child identify and communicate feelings affecting characters in relation to others? Does she show insight into her own problems and/or those of others?

7 Does the child show a capacity to take on imaginative roles? Does he show a variety of ways of interacting?

8 Does the child initiate ideas or lack confidence to use her own ideas?

Control of affect (expression of feelings)

1 How well does the child cope with being in a group?

2 Does the child show patience or tolerance in sharing adult attention, and sharing his possessions with sibling(s), or toys and equipment with peers?

3 Has the child an ability to sustain friendships?

4 Does the child co-operate with parents/carers and teachers?

5 Does the child show greater recognition of social signals and respond appropriately to her expressions of feelings?

6 Does the child name and share his own feelings?

7 Has the child's ability to sustain eye contact improved?

8 Have tantrums or anti-social behaviour increased or reduced?

9 Does the child show enjoyment of play?

Health and self-care

1 Has the child's visible appearance improved, e.g. their posture, or the tidiness and cleanliness of clothes, face and hands?

2 Has bowel control improved (where this is or has been an issue)?

3 Does the child (with previous eating difficulties) eat a wider variety of foods (within normal parameters)?

4 Have sleep problems reduced or are they spoken about more openly?

5 Have toileting problems – enuresis, soiling or constipation – been alleviated?

6 Have past incidents of self-harming behaviours or low mood reduced?

7 Does the traumatised child appear less hyper-vigilant?

Progress in school

1 Is the child working to higher levels of academic achievement?

2 Has the child's concentration level improved?

3 Is the child using imagination and more complex thought processing?

4 Does the child exhibit more enthusiasm and pleasure in her work?

5 Does the child show willingness and courage to try new activities?

6 Is he better able to make and keep friends without controlling them?

Relationships at home

1 Does the child talk more coherently and willingly about the past?

2 Is the child better able to think before acting on impulse?

3 Does the child show a desire to be helpful and co-operative?

4 Does the child share attention and have fewer arguments with siblings?

5 Is the child more inclined to give and receive affection?

6 Is there a reduction in stealing or compulsive lying?

7 Are traumatised children more able to manage their fear?

8 Have fidgeting, frequency of tantrums and fights reduced?

9 Does the child seek help and advice from adults more appropriately?

Evaluation of the "Theatre of Attachment" model

This model has not been formally validated; however, the evaluation forms completed by children and parents, and progress reports and observations by involved professionals, have contributed to the following formulations, based on work over the past ten years with 160 children placed in 140 adoptive and long-term foster families. First, let us take a look at why and when this intervention is required

Pre-intervention

Parents reported that when the children first came to live with them, they presented as having no imagination or ability to play properly with their toys. They experienced their children's frustrations, mainly expressed in withdrawal or lengthy tantrums, as immensely wearing, disenchanting and rejecting. After the first few weeks, many children had started to "push their luck".

Rude and non-compliant behaviour was attributed mainly to children's low self-esteem. Traumatised children were said to have problems with sleep, hygiene, and bowel control, and several had hidden their messy underclothes. Some had prowled the house at night, banging doors and searching for food. Most had found it difficult to enjoy treats or outings and, in their parents' view, seemed to deliberately undermine their efforts to give them a good time.

Other problems included social immaturity and lack of awareness of danger. The demands made by the children led to withdrawal of support promised by family and friends prior to placement, thus leaving adoptive parents, as well as their children, feeling socially isolated and blamed for these difficulties.

Post-intervention

Children were invited to complete a form asking them to write or draw their perception of why they thought they had been referred, what they liked or did not like about the intervention and what they hoped would happen next.

Changes in children

The children's perceptions: In response to being asked 'Why did you have therapy?', most replied, 'to help me' or to 'make me behave better', revealing their belief that they had been the cause of the problem. All commented positively on or drew happy images of the activities, which they enjoyed and wanted more of. Many of the younger children drew love hearts or images of themselves holding hands with a parent or, in some cases, with the therapist.

Analysis: It was apparent from the children's verbal accounts that physically re-enacting events from the past, within the safety of therapeutic play, enabled them to realise that they had not caused the problems leading to their being taken into care. This helped them to stop blaming themselves for what had been outside their control. Many children said things like: 'I used to hate myself. Now I feel like a hero. I feel like I belong.'

The creation of stories helps children initiate new ways for their own life story to evolve. Sequences in the stories improve their understanding of cause and effect ('I did this and here is the result'). The fictional freedom afforded by "magic" encourages children to aim forwards and find solutions to their dilemmas since stories can be given a resolution whereas problems in real life can frequently remain unresolved.

The children developed more complex thought processes, increasing their capacity to be coherent, make decisions and to reach satisfactory, credible resolutions. They gained an understanding of the need to be safe, enabled by parents taking roles that gave them the opportunity to ask their children, 'You know how it feels! So what should I do? Can you help me?' In response, children dispensed wisdom that they had been unaware of having possessed. This enhanced their self-esteem and resulted in a reduction of aggressive and anti-social patterns due to their feeling calmer and more in control of their feelings.

Changes in parents

Parents completed a questionnaire which asked them if and how their child had changed. Answers to ten questions on the areas of potential development were given on a scale of four choices, with space for further comments.

Parents reported having more energy and of gaining pleasure from seeing their children exert greater self-control. Many reported being thrilled to receive compliments from a teacher on the progress of their child, previously identified as a problem, and being proud when their child had been asked to befriend another troubled student. Some parents commented on how relieved and delighted they were at having their child seek them out to talk about feelings and worries. Knowing what troubles their children helps parents feel more confident to give the required reassurance. One parent reflected: 'Now I have the daughter I always wanted'. Another said the story involving water representing love had been a powerful turning point for his son who had previously been stuck in anger: 'He's happier, and I'm happier – it's outstanding the way this play therapy developed his creativity.' Parents reported that storytelling and creative play, alongside life history work, helped children to realise why they were living with their new parents as it had helped them to express themselves. Playing with clay had relaxed one child so much that she had become less aggressive, resulting in her parent feeling less afraid. This parent commented: 'Explaining what happened helped – it stopped her being so overwhelmed, though we're not out of the woods yet…'

One adoptive parent said of her son: 'He's proud to be part of our family and I feel more confident that we've done the right thing adopting him.' Another said, 'We have fun, we dance to the radio, we play football, do junk modelling and we read a lot together – they love stories, can't get enough of them; it's very rewarding and they are making nicer friends – that helps.'

Analysis: Parents who felt their child had changed for the better revealed how their own feelings had altered during the course of this work in the way they talked about, as well as to, their children. Gaining a deeper understanding of the impact of trauma and neglect on the developing brain enabled them to recognise the age at which their child was functioning moment to moment. Learning to observe body language (for example, a seven-year-old strutting in the manner of a pre-school infant) helped parents to anticipate difficulties and prepare the child in advance for likely triggers (such as coping with bossy peers or a cross teacher). Undertaking the life history work together gave parents the opportunity to reassure children that they were staying no matter what, which really helped to cement their relationship. Parents saw that the children loved dressing up as their birth parents and foster carers.

The children gained insights that reduced their anger towards birth parents for having rejected them. It helped some to become more tolerant of a sibling they had perceived as favoured. Parents were better able to resolve sibling rivalry by giving the older child appropriately enhanced status such as a later bedtime, and by ensuring that both received the individual attention they needed. They began to perceive their children as calmer and more accepting of their situation. 'We work hard at reassuring them and it's paying off.'

Conclusion

Children benefit from play with parents who replicate the mirroring relationship in which mothers engage with their infants during the first year of life. Once they feel relieved of self-blame, children with empathetic parents heal and flourish. Following the life history intervention, children feel freer to express a whole range of feelings, including anger and frustration.

Realising the significance of creative play in stimulating their children's imagination and problem-solving strategies encourages parents to engage more enthusiastically in play at the right level (such as floor play with young children). Age-related creative activities stimulate development while enhanced understanding leads parents to show greater patience in setting and enforcing realistic limits appropriate to the child's need.

Appendix:
Guide to empathic communication

We learn empathy from having it modelled for us by our parents. Neglected children who may not have learned empathy need adults to show caring attitudes, to demonstrate how to "step into another's shoes", and "see through someone else's eyes" in order to recognise their own and other's feelings. We all need to find out how we feel about varying aspects of life and relationships so that we can act on our feelings appropriately.

Under stress, traumatised children are easily overwhelmed by shame, fear, anger and embarrassment. To assess the emotional age of the behaviour they are displaying, it is helpful to observe their body language, movements and tone of voice (for example, a scared two-year-old might "erupt" and four-year-olds may fabricate).

The following responses are to enable parents to show they understand their child's feelings and that they want to help them find their own solutions.

Situations

It's raining heavily but the child wants to go outside to play.

The parent says:

'I wish we could go out! What would you do if you could?'

Perhaps the child wants to ride in his car.

'Let's see if we can make a car indoors!' (Use chairs)

The child says that no one will play with her.

Reflect how she feels about it:

'You feel no one cares! I know that feeling. I feel so sad for you! Thank you for telling me about it. I wonder what might help you find a friend.'

At the supermarket, your child keeps begging you to buy her sweets.

Acknowledge her craving:

'It would be lovely to eat lots and lots of sweets! But it's Mummy's (or Daddy's) job to look after your teeth. When you've helped me with this shopping, we'll make a plan to have something special.'

In public, the child keeps pretending she's a dog and insists on being addressed as such.

Say to your partner:

'She has a wonderful imagination! I'm playing her game today!' (This helps to distinguish "play" from "reality".)

Encourage your child to experiment with being a different animal and when she does, praise her:

'It's so much more fun playing with Horse!'

Get books about the new animal to encourage your child to find out how to care for it.

The child storms in, slamming doors, shouting.

The parent says:

'Wow, you're so good at letting me know how mad you are! I see that something's upset you! It's OK to feel mad but it's not OK to hurt people. I wonder who hurt you. I see how that worries you. It's happened to me too, it feels so awful.'

Later, if and when child is ready:

'Let me hug that cross feeling away!'

The child knocks over an object he's made at school. It breaks. The child flies into a rage, saying, *'It's your fault. You made me do it!'*

The parent says:

'You must be very disappointed that it broke. Maybe you're scared I'll blame you and get angry.'

If the child has suffered trauma, say:

'I wonder if you often got blamed for things that weren't your fault. I know you are scared. It makes me sad that such horrid things happened to you. But you are safe with me.'

Child rubbishes or destroys their work when their efforts don't succeed instantly.

The parent says: *'It's so frustrating when things don't work out! You had such a great idea. Scientists would know how you feel! They often experiment hundreds of times before getting the right formula!'*

When the child is ready, say: *'I wonder if you would like some more paper? Maybe you can try another way. I'm happy to help if I can, and just think how thrilled your teacher will be!'*

A brother complains that his sister has taken his chocolate bar. His sister's sleeve is covered in chocolate but she insists she hasn't had any of it.

The parent says:

'Your mouth is telling me one thing but your eyes say something else! I see by your cuffs you must have wanted that chocolate so badly, it really wasn't fair of me to make you wait so long for your share! But it's tough on him too! He was looking forward to it. What shall we do to make it up to him?'

Your daughter has brought home a pencil case that you don't recognise. On admiring it, you see a pencil inscribed with another child's name.

The parent says:

'I see this has your friend's name on it! You must have wanted that pencil case so badly. It's really hard when everyone else has such nice stuff. I guess you were thinking that she doesn't need it as much as you do!'

When the child admits it's not her pencil case, explain: *'You have to give this back. Let's work out when you'll have saved enough money to buy one like this for yourself!'*

Perhaps your child can be given tasks in exchange for a small financial reward to earn the desired object.

Children keep helping themselves to food from the cupboard.

Acknowledge this as a past survival mechanism. Promise them:

'You will never go hungry in this house. If you want food you only have to ask me.'

Your child tells tales to get other children into trouble.

Ask:

'I wonder how telling me about that child makes you feel?'

The child teases other children unkindly.

Let him hear you say to your partner:

'He hasn't learned how to make this fun yet!'

Praise and reward children who are acting in a socially competent way:

'I like it so much when you're having fun!'

Give encouraging messages, with sincerity (especially admire their efforts):

'I'm so proud of you! You're such a lovely person! I'm enjoying this activity, and being with you! I really appreciate how helpful you've been, thank you for being so patient when I was on the phone / shopping / etc.

When things go wrong and children get scared, remind them that when it happened before, they were too young to protect themselves. Now they are older, they can get help more easily. Reassure them you will always want them, no matter what.

Bibliography

Ainsworth M (1978) *Patterns of Attachment: A psychological study of the Strange Situation,* Hillsdale, NJ: Lawrence Erlbaum Associates

Annaz D, Karmiloff-Smith A and Thomas M (2008) 'The importance of tracing developmental trajectories for clinical child neuropsychology', in Warner-Rogers J and Reed J (eds) *Child Neuropsychology: Concepts, theory and practice,* Chichester: Wiley Blackwell

Balbernie R and Glaser D (2001) 'Early experience, attachment and the brain', in Gordon R and Harran E (eds) *Fragile – Handle with Care,* London: NSPCC

Baron-Cohen S and Chakrabarti B (2008) 'Social neuroscience', in Warner-Rogers J and Reed J (eds) *Child Neuropsychology: Concepts, theory and practice*, Chichester: Wiley Blackwell

Barratt S (2006) 'Kinship care: family stories, loyalties and binds', in Kenrick J, Lindsey C and Tollemache L (2006) *Creating New Families: Therapeutic approaches to fostering, adoption and kinship care*, London: Karnac

Bettelheim B (1979) *The Uses of Enchantment: The meaning and importance of fairy tales,* Harmondsworth: Penguin

Boal A (1995) *The Rainbow of Desire: The Boal method of theatre and therapy*, London: Routledge

Bowlby J (1973) *The Making and Breaking of Affectional Bonds*, London: Tavistock

Bowlby J and Ainsworth M (1962) 'The effects of maternal deprivation: a review of findings and controversy in the context of research strategy', *Public Health Papers*, no. 14, Geneva: World Health Organization

Brocklesby E, Le Vaillant J, McCormick A, Mandelli D and Mather M (2009) 'Substance misuse in pregnancy: an unrecognised and misdiagnosed problem for a child', *Seen and Heard,* 19:1, pp. 22–32

Cattanach A (1999) *Process in the Arts Therapies,* London: Jessica Kingsley Publishers

Collishaw S, Pickles A, Messer J, Rutter M, Shearer C and Maughan B (2007) cited by Rushton (2010) 'Thinking on developmental psychology in fostering and adoption', *Adoption & Fostering*, 34:3, pp. 38–43

Corrigan M and Moore J (2011) *Listening to Children's Wishes and Feelings*, London: BAAF

Cowan N, Hamilton Z, Towze J, Hitch G, Scott Saults J, Elliott E, Lacey J and Moreno M (2003) 'Children's working memory processes: a response timing analysis', *Journal of Experimental Psychology*, 132:1, pp. 113–132

Cozolino L (2006) *The Neuroscience of Human Relationships: Attachment and the developing brain,* New York: Norton

Crittenden P (2009) *Raising Parents: Attachment, parenting and child safety,* Cullompton, Devon, Willan Publishing

Damasio A (1998) 'Emotion in the perspective of an integrated nervous system', *Brain Research Reviews,* 26, pp. 83–86

Damasio A (2001) 'Fundamental feelings', *Nature*, 412, p. 781

Dance C and Rushton A (2005) 'Predictors of outcomes for unrelated adoptive placements made during middle childhood', *Child and Family Social Work*, 10, pp. 269–280

Erikson E (1963) *Childhood and Society* (2nd edn), New York, NY: Norton

Fonagy P (2009) 'Psychoanalytic psychotherapy as an evidence-based practice: keynote presentation to the British Psychoanalytic Council Spring Conference', *Psychoanalytic Psychotherapy Now* conference, London

Fonagy P, Leigh T, Steele M, Steele H, Kennedy R, Mattoon, G, Target M and Gerber A (1996) 'The relation of attachment status, psychiatric classification, and response to psychotherapy', *Journal of Consulting and Clinical Psychology*, 64, pp. 22–31

Fraiberg V (ed) (2008) *The Magic Years*, London: Scribner

Freud S (1948) *Beyond the Pleasure Principle*, London: HBDJ Hogarth

Geddes H (2006) *Attachment in the Classroom: The links between children's early experience, emotional well-being and performance in school: A practical guide for schools*, London: Jessica Kingsley Publishers

Gersie A and King N (1990) *Storymaking in Education and Therapy*, London: Jessica Kingsley Publishers

Goosens S (1997) 'Brecht, Jones and Artaud', available at: www.studyworld.com

Grotowski J (1975) 'Towards a Poor Theatre', cited in Slowiak J and Cuesta J, *Jerzy Growowski*, New York, NY: Routledge

Harlow HE (1951) 'Primate learning', in Stone CP (ed) *Cognitive Psychology*, New York: Prentice Hall, pp. 185–238

Hester M (2011) 'The Three Planet Model: towards an understanding of contradictions in approaches to women's and children's safety in contexts of domestic violence', *British Journal of Social Work,* 41, pp. 837–853

Hogarth L and Comfort H (2010) *A Practical Guide to Outcome Evaluation*, London: Jessica Kingsley Publishers

Howard-Jones P (2008) 'From brain scan to lesson plan', *Neuroeducation*, 24:2, pp. 110–113

Howard-Jones P, Winfield M and Crimmins G (2008) 'Co-constructing an understanding of creativity in drama education that draws on neuropsychological concepts', *Educational Research*, 50:2, pp. 187–201

Hughes D (2006) *Building the Bonds of Attachment: Awakening love in deeply troubled children* (2nd ed) New York, NY: Jason Aronson

Ironside L (2004) 'Living a provisional existence: thinking about foster carers and the emotional containment of children placed in their care', *Adoption & Fostering,* 28:4, pp. 39–49

Jennings S (ed) (2009) *Dramatherapy and Social Theatre: Necessary dialogues,* Hove, East Sussex: Routledge

Jennings S (2011) *Neuro-Dramatic Play,* London: Jessica Kingsley Publishers

Jewett C (1984) *Helping Children Cope with Separation and Loss*, London: BAAF/Batsford

Jones CL, Rosencrantz K, Rothwell JC and Jehenshashad M (2004) 'The right dorsolateral pre-frontal cortex is essential in time reproduction: an investigation with repetitive transcranial magnetic stimulus', *Experimental Brain Research*, 158:3, pp. 366–72

Jung C (1968) *Archetypes and the Collective Unconscious*, London: Routledge

Kawakami N, Shimizu H, Haratani T, Iwata N and Kitamurae T (2004) 'Lifetime and six-month prevalence of DSM III-R psychiatric conditions in an urban community in Japan', *Psychiatry Research*, 121, pp. 293–301

Kenrick J, Lindsey C and Tollemache L (eds) (2006) *Creating New Families: Therapeutic approaches to fostering, adoption and kinship care*, London: Karnac

Kessler R, Berglund P, Demler O, Jin R, Koretz D, Merikangas K, Rush A, Walters E and Wang P (2003) 'The epidemiology of major depressive disorder: results from the National Comorbidity Survey Replication', *Journal of American Medical Association*, 289, pp. 3095–3105

Kolb B, Gorny G, Li Y, Samaha A and Robinson T (2003) 'Amphetamine or cocaine limits the ability of later experience to promote structural plasticity in the neo cortex and nucleus acumbens', *Proceedings of the National Academy of Sciences*, 100, pp. 10523–10528

Kraus N (2010) *Cognitive-Sensory Interaction in the Neural Encoding of Music and Speech*, Evanston, IL: North Western University, American Association for the Advancement of Science

Lacher D, Nichols T and May J (2005) *Connecting with Kids through Stories: Using narrative to facilitate attachment in adopted children*, London: Jessica Kingsley Publishers

Lahad M (2000) *Creative Supervision*, London: Jessica Kingsley Publishers

Landy R (2001) *New Essays in Drama Therapy: Unfinished business*, Springfield, IL: Charles C Thomas Publishers

Le Doux J (1998) *The Emotional Brain: The mysterious underpinnings of emotional life*, London: Phoenix

Le Vay D (2011) 'Journey into the interior: narrative play therapy with young people who sexually harm', in Taylor de Faoite A (ed) *Narrative Play Therapy: Theory and practice*, London: Jessica Kingsley Publishers

Lehrer J (2009) *How we Decide*, New York, NY: Mariner

MacIntyre A (1985) *After Virtue: A study in moral theory* (2nd edn) Paris: University of Notre Dame Press

Main M, Kaplan N and Cassidy J (1985) 'Security in infancy, childhood and adulthood: a move to the level of representation', *Monographs of the Society for Research in Child Development*, 50, pp. 66–104

Moore J (2006) '"Theatre of Attachment": using drama to facilitate attachment in adoption', *Adoption & Fostering*, 30:2, pp. 64–73

Moore J (2008) '"Theatre of Attachment": use of drama in adoption/foster families', in Jennings S (ed) (2009) *Dramatherapy and Social Theatre: Necessary dialogues*, Chichester: Routledge

Moore J (2010) 'A story to tell: use of story and drama in work with substitute families', *Journal of Dramatherapy*, 31:3, pp. 3–9

Moreno J (1946), cited in Courtney R (1995) *Drama and Feeling: An aesthetic theory*, Montreal: McGill Queen's University Press

Morrison M (2012) *Talking about Adoption to your Adopted Child* (4th edn), London: BAAF

Mukherjee R (2009) *FASD Diagnosis and Neurodevelopmental Outcomes*, London: University of London

Murphy E (2007) 'Images of children in mothers' accounts of contemporary childrearing', *Childhood*, 14, pp. 105–126

O'Connor MJ and Paley B (2006), cited in Keenan T and Evans S (2009) *An Introduction to Child Development* (2nd edn) London: Sage

Pennebaker JW and Seagal JD (1999) 'Forming a story: the health benefits of narrative', *Journal of Clinical Psychology*, 55, pp. 1243–54

Perry B (2009) 'Examining child maltreatment through a neurodevelopmental lens: clinical applications of the neurodevelopmental model of therapeutics', *Journal of Loss and Trauma*, 14, pp. 240–255

Perry B and Pollard R (1998) 'Homeostasis, stress, trauma and adaptation: a neurodevelopmental view of childhood trauma', *Child and Adolescent Psychiatric Clinics of North America,* 7:1, pp. 22–46

Perry B and Szalavitz M (2006) *The Boy who was Raised as a Dog and Other Stories from a Child Psychiatrist's Notebook: What traumatised children can teach us about loss, love and healing*, New York, NY: Basic Books

Robinson K (2001) *Out of our Minds: Learning to be creative*, Oxford: Capstone Publishing

Rushton A (2003) *The Adoption of Looked After Children: A scoping review of research*, London: Social Care Institute for Excellence/Policy Press

Rushton A (2010) 'Thinking on developmental psychology in fostering and adoption', *Adoption & Fostering*, 34:3, pp.38–43

Russ S (2004) *Play in Child Development and Psychotherapy: Toward empirically supported practice*, New York, NY: Lawrence Erbaum Associates

Russ S and Niec L (eds) (2011) *Play in Clinical Practice*, New York, NY: Guilford Press

Schore A (2006) *Affect Dysregulation and Disorders of the Self*, London: Norton

Selekman M (1997) *Solution-Focussed Therapy with Children: Harnessing family strengths for systemic change*, New York, NY: Guilford Press

Selekman M (2005) *Pathways to Change: Brief therapy with difficult adolescents*, New York, NY: Guilford Press

Selwyn J (2010) 'The challenges in planning for permanency', *Adoption & Fostering*, 34:3, pp 32–37

Selwyn J, Sturgess W, Quinton D and Baxter C (2006) *Costs and Outcomes of Non-Infant Adoptions*, London: BAAF

Sherborne V (1991) *Developmental Movement for Children*, Richmond: Worth Publishing

Siegel D (1999) *The Developing Mind*, New York, NY: Guilford Press

Slade P (1954) *Child Drama,* London: Norton

Sroufe A, Egeland B, Carlson E and Andrew Collins W (2005) *The Development of the Person: The Minnesota study of risk and adaptation from birth to adulthood*, New York, NY: Guildford Press

Sunderland M (2007) *The Neuroscience of Attachment,* conference paper, Bedford, 31 March 2007

Teicher MH, Samson JA, Polcari A and McGreenery CE (2006) 'Sticks, stones and hurtful words: relative effects of various forms of childhood maltreatment', *American Journal of Psychiatry*, 163:6, pp. 993–1000

Todd R and Lewis M (2008) 'Self regulation in the developing brain', in Warner-Rogers J and Reed J (eds) *Child Neuropsychology: Concepts, theory and practice*, Chichester: Wiley Blackwell

Van der Kolk B, McFarlane A and Weisaeth L (eds) (2007) *Traumatic Stress: The effects of overwhelming experience on mind, body and society,* New York, NY: Guilford

Verrier N (2010) (UK edn) *Coming Home to Self: Healing the primal wound*, London: BAAF

Von Franz M (1996) *The Interpretation of Fairy Tales*, Boston, MA: Shambhala Publications

Warner-Rogers J and Reed J (eds) (2008) *Child Neuropsychology: Concepts, theory and practice*, Chichester: Wiley Blackwell

White M (2007) *Maps of Narrative Practice*, New York, NY: Norton

Willett J (1977) *The Theatre of Bertolt Brecht*, London: Methuen

Winnicott D (1971) *Playing and Reality*, London: Tavistock

Wolfs R (2009) *Adoption Conversations*, London: BAAF

Wolfs R (2010) *More Adoption Conversations*, London: BAAF

Acknowledgements

I want to thank the adoptive and foster parents and their children who have helped to create many of these wonderful stories. I have taken care to protect their confidentiality and to be sensitive to cultural issues. I also thank the supporting social workers with whom I have had the pleasure to work.

For their invaluable advice and moral support, my thanks go to my supervisor, Professor Sue Jennings, and my colleagues who read sections of this book and have given such positive feedback. These include Fran Taylor, Mary Corrigan, Jo Williams, Linda Hoggan, Diane Hanlon, Angela Lawton, Pene Sinnot, Caroline High, Rundeep Sembi, Jean Francois Jacques, and Jay Vaughan who has so generously written the foreword to this book. Special thanks also to Hedi Argent who read, edited and commented on an early draft.

My thanks also go to Shaila Shah and the publishing team at BAAF for their efforts on my behalf. Last but not least, I thank my husband and our two children for their enduring and precious love and encouragement.

Note about the author

Joan Moore is a freelance Adoption Support Agency, dramatherapist, play therapist, trainer, and registered supervisor with over thirty years' experience in social work. During the past 12 years of therapeutic work with foster and adoptive families, influenced by her research into the neuroscience of child development, attachment, neglect and trauma, she has developed her method of storytelling alongside her "Theatre of Attachment" model which involves adoptive parents in performing plays of their children's life history.

Joan also undertakes play and dramatherapy in schools, court assessments, and delivers training in direct work for local authorities, plus the adoption and assessment modules of the MA programme for Therapia.

Having written several articles, Joan is co-author with Mary Corrigan of the BAAF (2011) training programme and handbook, *Listening to Children's Wishes and Feelings*. Joan's forthcoming book, *Emotional Problem Solving using Stories, Drama and Play*, due to be published by Hinton House in 2012, addresses issues such as bullying, low self-esteem, sibling rivalry, disability, and bereavement, all issues that affect a wider population of children.

www.adoptedchildtherapyservice.co.uk/